WHAT PEOPLE ARE SAYING ABOUT THIS BOOK

"I am thrilled to add **The Illinois Road Guide to Haunted Locations** *to my eclectic library. Our hometown hero, Popeye, will need to stock up on some fortifying spinach before he dares to finish the tome!"*

Michael W. McClure- Popeye Picnic Chairman and author of the *SeaHag History & Mystery Tours*

****

"City by city, county by county, bring this guide with you and come explore the dark, haunted side of our grand state."

Scott Maruna- Swamp Gas Books

D0675153

THE
ILLINOIS
ROAD GUIDE
TO
HAUNTED
LOCATIONS

Library Readers:
Good luck on your
ghost adventure!

THE
ILLINOIS
ROAD GUIDE
TO
HAUNTED
LOCATIONS

By Chad Lewis & Terry Fisk

UNEXPLAINED
Research Publishing Company
A Division of Unexplained Research, LLC

Fx: 5-09

Library of Congress Control Number: 2006903790
ISBN: 978-0-9762099-5-9

Printed in the United States by Documation

Unexplained Research Publishing Company
A Division of Unexplained Research LLC
P.O. Box 2173, Eau Claire, WI 54702-2173
Email: info@unexplainedresearch.com
www.unexplainedresearch.com

Cover Design: Terry Fisk
Back Cover Photo: Rob Mattison

DEDICATION

I dedicate this book to Sherrie Lewis for the love and life she shared with my dad for many years.

—Chad

Dedicated to the Amnicon Brothers. The Amnicon Seniors (Arlan "Hootie" Jones, Rick "Axe" Fisk, & Steve "Jazz" Clark), Amnicon Juniors (Chuck Boyce-Fisk, Jeremy Jones, Niles Boyce-Fisk, Jason Holm, Jordan Fisk, & Jordan Jones), and "Amnicon the Next Generation" (Anthony, Drake, & Colton Boyce-Fisk).

—Terry

TABLE OF CONTENTS

2 - Chicago Illinois   **75**

PREFACE

Corrections. Although we have made every effort to be certain this road guide is reliable and accurate, things inevitably change and errors are made. We appreciate it when readers contact us so we can revise future editions of the book.

Updates. If you have a paranormal experience at one of these locations, please report it to us. We recommend that you keep a journal, carefully recording dates, times, locations, and what happened.

Additions. Due to lack of space, many locations had to be left out the book. We do intend to publish a second volume. Please write and let us know of any Illinois locations that you feel should have been included in this travel guide.

Warning. Be respectful of both the living and the dead. Several communities have had problems with people who go to these locations only to party and cause mischief. Cemeteries have been desecrated; private property has been vandalized; grounds have been littered; and buildings have been broken into.

If you do decide to check out any of the locations for yourself, please make sure that you have permission if it is private property and obey all applicable laws. Under most ordinances, cemeteries are only open from sunrise to sunset.

We will not be held responsible for any persons who decide to conduct their own investigations or for those who choose to break laws.

Disclaimer. The places listed in the book have neither been proved nor disproved to be haunted. Their inclusion in the book is based on the anecdotal reports we have received from numerous individuals. This book is for reference purposes only.

FOREWORD

Confessions of an
Accidental (Paranormal) Tourist in Illinois

Oh, how I wish this book had been published ten or even twenty years ago! It has been said that 'Instances of true love are like ghosts; they are oft spoken of, but almost never seen'. Now, as much as I would like to say that this book could solve your love-life problems, it can not. However, it certainly can correct the deficiency mentioned in the other half of the proverb.

Care well for this book, for the tome which you are now holding is your ticket to advance from the haphazard status of "accidental paranormal tourist" (like myself) to the rank of expert Illinois ghost seeker. It is a ticket that I never possessed and thus, I am officially jealous of those who have such a head start. Utilized wisely, the user of this guidebook will surpass all of us seekers before you. For, as you will find, I had to stumble my way through "accidentally"—you will have a guide.

Allow me to elaborate briefly on my journey, not because you the reader care about my history, but rather because I hope to—along the way—convey and prove to you what a treasure trove of haunts and mysteries the state of Illinois truly is.

*****

I was born and raised in Charleston, Illinois, home of Eastern Illinois University. It was here as a child that I had my appetite for ghosts whetted with tales of the forlorn hauntings that occurred on the upper floor of Pemberton Hall on the university's campus. Only, my hometown was too "academic" to embrace the treasure it possessed in that now boarded-up and abandoned section of the former dormitory.

When I finally earned that passport to freedom—my driver's license, my passage into accidental paranormal tourism really commenced. It all began with short excursions into the "next town," Mattoon. Ostensibly, these jaunts were executed for practical reasons, such as shopping at the mall or catching the new-release movie, but the actual entertainment to be found here was the stash of accounts still told by the most senior of residents. Tales of a "phantom anesthetist" that terrorized the town for three weeks in September of 1944 by spraying a sickly-sweet gas into the windows of homes, paralyzing the horrified occupants abounded. No cause or culprit was ever located by authorities. Though many, including myself, have postulated upon the root of these attacks, it remains to this day one of the great unexplained mysteries of America.

When I set off as a young, green freshman bound for college at Western Illinois University in Macomb, Illinois, I was greeted by not one, but three allegedly haunted dorm rooms and a house in town that once accommodated one of the most celebrated fire-starting poltergeists anywhere—no doubt an inspiration for Steven King's *Fire Starter*.

I eventually transferred to MacMurray College in Jacksonville, Illinois where, while working part-time as a night security guard, I received a garbled call on my radio to get over to the student center immediately...the "blue lady" had just been sighted. Believed to be the ghost of a freshman coed jilted by a homecoming dance date who leapt to her death from her dorm window a century ago, the apparition has been seen on campus for three generations. Sadly, when I arrived on the scene, I found only a very flustered and disturbed young lady who could not accept what she had just witnessed. And the "blue lady" was just one of four ghosts whispered to haunt the tiny campus of eight hundred students.

After graduating with an honors degree in biology, I accepted a teaching assignment in one of the most remote spots in the state, Brussels, Illinois. It was here that my students told me about the phantom big black cats that roamed the hills and 'hollers of Calhoun County. "Impossible," I remember saying to them. "There are no cougars, let alone black panthers, east of the Mississippi." How wrong I was. Though, how could I have known it at the time? The state still refuses to accept that they are there...and perhaps, just perhaps, they are not. Are ghosts of the state's past predators still haunting the Illinois River Valley bottoms?

In time, I moved and took a teaching position in a school near the town of Farmer City. While here, I was confronted with stories of a giant, phantom ape-man—lovingly called the "Farmer City Monster"—that haunted the area in the 1970s. The locals still attest to the veracity of the witnesses and their testimony.

For a nine year stretch of my life following this, I moved more times than I care to remember and every time...you guessed it, an accidental paranormal tourist spot came into my life.

My next stop that I briefly called home was a bucolic area just north of Lincoln, Illinois. My teaching brought me in contact with Lincoln College and its multiple resident ghosts, while my work commute required daily trips past Middletown, Illinois' 400th Avenue Bridge, which is supposed to be one of the state's most illustrious of out-of-doors haunted locations. I stopped many a time...again—to the passing drivers—apparently for rest, but I knew otherwise. Also on my daily route was a little hamlet named Lawndale. It was here in 1977 that little Marlon Lowe was seized and carried several feet through the air by a giant bird of a size unheard of in Illinois or anywhere else in the Midwest. Mystery was everywhere I looked.

My next move took me to Havana, Illinois where I became loosely associated with a thespian troupe that owned an aged theatre that once served as a vaudevillian stage and later as an early home of silent movies and "talkies." Though vacant for many years, the theater was anything but empty. The building owner told me of the multiple encounters he had with the specter of a former stage manager from the turn of the century, who appears corporally in the basement recurrently, only to vanish into thin air.

Within a year, I was back in Jacksonville in the teaching position that I have now held for eleven years. In just a few short years though, I collected enough legends and yarns of local ghosts and haunts to fill and eventually become the subject matter of my third book.

*****

Again, honestly, my life story is inconsequential. It is what accompanied that story that still astounds me as I look back upon it. In a matter of almost forty years, I stumbled—purely by accident—into ghostly and phantasmal locales and places at every single stop, in every single year and in every venue that the realm of the paranormal offers. For a time, I became paranoid and almost convinced that some unseen force was guiding me from haunted situation to haunted situation everywhere I went. However, the solution to this mystery-life of mine was far more veiled and prosaic: I lived in Illinois.

It took me a long time, loads of research and numerous relocations within this beautiful state to fully come to terms with just how many exceptional haunted locations could be found everywhere throughout the state. Illinois is a weird place! And what has that realization made me want? More. More haunted buildings, more haunted cemeteries, more haunted roads and woods in Illinois. MORE!

But...I don't want to move anymore (no matter how much U-Haul loves me)! I want the next forty years to be filled with controlled paranormal tourism. I haven't even gotten to the Chicago area as a paranormal tourist at all (outside of the rare cursed-Cubs game) and do you know how many ghostly sites are in the windy city alone? You will, when you are finished with this book. This book is the key to your and my next weekend getaway, your next vacation, your next business trip (Have to go to Peoria for the day? Your must-see stop on the way is in here!).

City by city, county by county, bring this guide with you and come explore the dark, haunted side of our grand state.

Scott Maruna
News Editor, Anomalist.com
Author of *The Mad Gasser of Mattoon: Dispelling the Hysteria, The History and Mystery of the Piasa Bird* and *The Unexplained Mysteries of Jacksonville.*
www.swampgasbooks.com

ACKNOWLEDGMENTS

We would like to thank Nisa Giaquinto, Sarah Szymanski, Amber Boyce-Fisk, and Jeannine Fisk for assisting us with the research and production of this book.

We also want to thank the many people who provided us with cases, directions, and personal accounts.

INTRODUCTIONS

Thanks to the Interstate Highway System, it is now possible to travel from coast to coast without seeing anything.

—Charles Kuralt

The Illinois Bureau of Tourism provides an endless array of exciting activities you can partake in while visiting or living in Illinois. If you are an avid sports fan, you have a wide choice of teams to cheer for. During any given season you could find yourself cheering for the Bears, Blackhawks, Bulls, Cubs, or Sox. If sports are not your thing, you could choose to spend the day in the audience for a taping of Oprah's talk show. If a slower paced weekend is more your style, you could certainly spend a quiet relaxing evening with your loved one in a cozy bed and breakfast overlooking the river. Don't forget about antiquing, biking, fishing, hiking, hunting, museums, and the theater. This list could go on and on forever. There are so many activities to participate in you could literally stay busy for years.

But what if you want to venture off the path in search of something a bit weirder than the norm? Well lucky for you Illinois provides plenty of opportunities to quench the thirst of even the most die-hard adventurer. It is the state where you can come face to face with the ghost of the notorious gangster John Dillinger, or you can pay your respects to the dead while attending a phantom funeral. It is the state where you can hear the eerie sounds of a violin being played by the ghostly spirit of a young girl, while still having plenty of time in your day to visit a "haunted" haunted house.

Rest assured, this guide makes visiting all of these places easy. We took care of all the hard work. We scoured the old records for the real history of the place, dug up the ghost lore, recorded the eyewitness accounts, conducted our own investigation, and captured photos of the site. We even provide you with directions on how to get there. However, part of this book is just like the old "choose your own adventures," as we have left the biggest choice up to you. Do you want to read about these cases from the safety of your own home, or would you rather visit these places for yourself? But please beware, going to these places is much different from watching them on TV, because when you're in a haunted cemetery and you see a shadowy figure lurking from gravestone to gravestone, you cannot simply change the channel, and when you hear the unearthly moans from children eternally trapped at their place of death, the mute button will do you no good.

Maybe you are the type of person who likes to heed warnings and you have decided to skip visiting all of these places and would prefer to sit back in the safety of your favorite reading chair and enjoy these stories with a nice cup of hot chocolate. Of course, by choosing this route you might just miss out on being chased through the Ramsey woods and caves by a werewolf, and you would never know if the Gates to Hell really provided a portal to the underworld. My advice is to pack this book, grab a friend, and take the cocoa to go, as you begin your own haunted adventure. This is your chance to get out and truly explore the state. Trust me, while you are on this adventure you will meet some odd people, see many strange things, uncover local lore, and discover that Illinois is much more exciting and bizarre than you could have ever imagined, and you may just find that you are too.

Keep an eye out,

Chad Lewis

Do the thing you fear and the death of fear is certain.

—Ralph Waldo Emerson

It was during the Great Depression, shortly after the Saint Valentine's Day Massacre, that my grandparents met in Chicago. Grandpa Harry had moved down from Wisconsin to manage a White Castle hamburger restaurant and Grandma Scottie had moved from Indiana to attend nursing school. I'm not sure of the details of how they met and fell in love, but I do know they got married in 1935 in Cook County, and my father Larry was born in Chicago the following year. It was a time when Chicago bootleggers and gangsters were making the headlines. My grandmother had finished her schooling and when grandpa's store was robbed at gunpoint, he decided it was best to move the family to a small down in northwestern Wisconsin, which is where I was later born and raised.

Because of my Illinois roots, I was eager to return to the Land of Lincoln to hear the stories and experiences that people had to share. This book is the fruition of that journey. As I drove across the state, I found travel guides telling me where to find lodging, restaurants, historic places, tourist places, etc., but the road guide you hold in your hands is a manual for finding the preternatural places of Illinois. It isn't meant to be a scientific treatise to convince closed-minded debunkers that a paranormal realm exists. Rather, it's written for those souls brave enough to be legend trippers. Every town has its legends and rumors of haunted locations, but often people don't know where to find these places. Here's your opportunity to not only explore Illinois, but to examine and challenge your inner self, your beliefs, and your courage.

Enjoy!

Terry Fisk

CENTRAL ILLINOIS

Saint Omer Cemetery

Location: Ashmore, Coles County, Illinois

Directions: From Ashmore take 2410 E to the north toward Oakland. At 2.5 miles, start to slow down, because you will see a small sign for the cemetery on your left, right next to a gravel path (1320N) St. Omer Rd. Follow the path to the cemetery.

Ghost Lore

Approximately every fours years, in order to keep our calendars in alignment with the earth's rotation around the sun we have a leap year. During these years, an additional day gets added to the month of February. Due to this additional day, it is not uncommon to have been born or to have died on February 29th. But have you ever heard of someone dying on February 31st? Visitors to St. Omer Cemetery certainly have, because buried deep within this remote cemetery is a gravestone of a witch that died on February 31st.

- Murdered for practicing witchcraft, the vengeful spirit of a woman haunts the cemetery.

- No matter how many times you try to take of picture of the crystal ball gravestone, it will not show up.

- At night, the usually dark cemetery is lit up with the eerie glowing of the mysterious tombstone.

History

1834 – Cutler's Settlement was established in the area.

1852 – According to the newsletter *Legends and Lore of Coles County, IL*, the town of St. Omer, which had been known as Cutler's Settlement, was officially established. However, according to the *History of Coles County, 1879*, St. Omer was never laid out as a village. It did have at one time a half a dozen homes, a store, a post office, and a blacksmith shop.

1859 – The township of Ashmore was established.

1881 – Marcus Barnes, Caroline's husband passed away.

1882 – Caroline Barnes passed away from pneumonia.

1869-1893 – The town of St. Omer appeared on local plot maps.

1893 – The Barnes family owned the land in which the cemetery now rests.

Investigation

The large crystal gravestone is actually a family burial plot. The orb and pyre gravestone marks the burial of four members from the Barnes family, including: Granvil, Sarah, Marcus, and Caroline.

The date of death carved on the stone of Caroline Barnes is indeed February 31, 1882. According to the newsletter *Legends and Lore of Coles County, IL,* there is some confusion as to the actual date of Caroline's Death. One document lists her death as taking place on February 26th, while another document lists the date of death as February 28th. One main theory explaining the mysterious date on

the tombstone claims that the wrong date was simply carved into the grave purely by mistake. By the time the blunder was discovered, the stone had already been carved. It was then decided that it would be too expensive to fix the error due to the prohibitive cost of a new monument.

Local lore tells that Caroline was murdered by conservative God-fearing members of the community, who believed that Caroline was a witch. Afraid that her dabbling into the dark arts might draw forth evil spirits upon town, a decision was made to murder her. We were unable to find any evidence suggesting that Caroline was a witch, or that she was murdered.

It is believed that the cursed gravestone will be visible to the naked eye, but will not show up on any photographs. However, while we were investigating the cemetery, we took numerous photos, all of which clearly show the gravestone.

A group of friends informed us that one evening they decided to drive out to the old cemetery to see the gravestone and experience the legend for themselves. While they were driving down the

entrance to the cemetery, they noticed a soft glow coming from the tombstone. The group commented that the glow was probably just the flashlights of others legend trippers that were also at the cemetery. Once the group got fully inside the cemetery they soon realized they were alone and that the phantom light had simply disappeared.

Burton Cave

Location: Burton, Adams County, Illinois

Directions (Caution—Very hard to find): From the town of Quincy, take State Rd. 6 miles to the east to the village of Burton. From State Rd., turn right on E 1350 (gravel road with a yellow house on the corner). Follow this road and you will come to a Y. Take the Y to the left toward the small bridge. Once you pass over the bridge you will encounter two Y's. Make sure to take the right path on each. The second right will lead you along a cornfield and in approximately ½ mile you will come to a lone large tree on your left. You can park there. Once you get out of your car, on your right, will be a path labeled "Illinois Nature Reserve Trail." Take this trail for about 100 yards along the bluffs (not the river) and you will run into the entrance of the cave. The main portion of the cave is sealed off to protect the bats.

Ghost Lore

There is an old mysterious cave hidden in the middle of nowhere that is haunted by several ghosts. Those who are brave enough to locate the cave often are never heard from again, because the spirits haunting the cave pull will pull you in and you will never see the light of day again.

- Strange stories of ghosts, vengeful spirits, and disappearing robed figures have been reported around the cave for many years.

- Although the cave area is tranquil and quiet during the day-time, at night the cave transforms into a sinister place that should be avoided at all costs.

History

1848 – The cave was said to be discovered by a local man. No name of the discoverer was given at the time.

1860 – It is believed that the area was mainly used as farmland by local pioneers.

1930s – To escape the blistering heat of the summer, many towns-folk from Quincy gathered up their pillows and set off to spend the night in the cool cave which stayed a constant 55-56 degrees.

1947 – Mrs. Ellen Tandy Hands told a reporter that her father, H.L. Tandy, was the one who originally discovered the cave. Apparently her father was 16 years old when he stumbled upon the cave in 1832.

1960 – The Quincy Foundation acquired the land from the Tandy family, which had owned and farmed the land since the 1800s.

1961 – The cave gained popularity with amateur spelunkers and explorers when it was featured in the publication *Caves of Illinois* by Bretz and Harris.

1966 – The Quincy Foundation donated the preserve to the Nature Conservancy.

1978 – Quincy College signed a ten-year agreement with the Nature Conservancy to study the cave. The college used the area as an outdoor laboratory for its students.

1981 – The Illinois Department of Conservation acquired the land and cave system from the Nature Conservancy.

1986 – Burton Cave was granted the title of Nature Preserve. The cave became the only cave in Illinois to receive the State Preserve recognition.

1997 – The Illinois Department of Natural Resources and Bat Conservation International, along with several local and national groups constructed a bat-friendly gate that closed off the main part of the cave to visitors.

Investigation

The mysterious cave mentioned in the ghost lore is an Illinois Nature Preserve called Burton Cave. The preserve is an 85-acre piece of land that houses the cave and surrounding land. Most of the inside of the cave is closed off to the public to protect both the Gray and Indiana bats that hibernate in the cave. Since both species of bat are endangered species, a gate was constructed to keep visitors from disturbing the creatures of the night. We were told by those living within a few miles of the cave that they can still see the bats coming out at night to feed.

Since the discovery of the cave, locals have told cautionary tales of curious explorers who would often go into the cave, but they would never come back.

In the 1800s, a small group of Quincy citizens set off to have a picnic near Burton Cave. After their picnic, they had plans to explore the cave. Unfortunately, severe weather conditions cut their picnic short, and they headed for shelter of the cave. As the group neared the cave, they were startled by a strange dark-robed figure that sprang out of the cave and simply disappeared before their eyes. Caught between their fear of the unknown figure and the pouring rain, the group pressed on into the cave. Once inside, the group noticed a faint glow emanating from inside the cave. Curious to find the cause of the glow, the group went to investigate. It didn't take long for the group to find the source of the light. The glow was coming from dozens of lit candles that were placed around the dead body of a woman in white lying on the ground. The witnesses thought that it looked as though a funeral or some type of bizarre ritual was taking place. The group was then getting scared and decided not to stick around to find out what was happening, as they tore off for the safety of the daylight. The sheriff was notified of the group's eerie find. The sheriff gathered up a couple of his deputies and set off for the cave. However, once the officers of the law got to the cave, they found no signs of a woman, candles, or mysterious robed figure. All evidence lead the officers to believe that no one had even been in the cave.

During the 1920s and 30s, many people used the area surrounding the cave for picnics. The damp cold cave area was also used to avoid the sweltering summer heat. With so many visitors to the area, the cave started to gain a reputation of being a mysterious place. Stories of the cave being haunted by several ghosts and spirits only added to the eeriness surrounding the area.

Rumors also spread when newspapers of the 1930s claimed that a bizarre hermit named John Clinginsmith lived alone in a 100-year-

old cabin near the cave. The hermit was said to be an eccentric man that possessed great mystical powers, including the ability to heal animals.

Reports of the cave and surrounding area gained even more popular exposure through Harry Hyatt's 1935 book *Folk-Lore From Adams County Illinois.* In the book, Hyatt describes the story of a man being killed outside of the cave. It was believed that if you made the mistake of getting too close to the cave at night "something" would pull you into the cave.

A man living in Burton told us that he heard a strange story about the cave from a neighbor of his who lived his whole life near the cave. The neighbor explained his explorations into the cave. He said that after passing though many small openings, you eventual-

ly come to a large room that has a hole in the floor. The man went on to say that the strange thing about the hole is that it is so deep that when you drop a rock, you can't hear it hit the bottom. Where the hole led to, the neighbor never said.

Today, many of the people we spoke with who live in the area around the cave still know of and believe the strange stories of the cave. However, to the many people in the nearby towns, the stories of the mysterious cave seems to have disappeared, much like those who have entered it.

The Witch's Grave

Location: Chesterville, Douglas County, Illinois

Directions: From Hwy 133 turn N on 425 E. Turn right on 370 N and follow it over the old iron bridge and the cemetery will be on your left-hand side.

Ghost Lore

Chesterville is a quite slow moving town filled with many small Amish and Mennonite communities. It is the exact type of place where you would expect to hear kids recite the timeless and universal phrase of "There is nothing to do here." Perhaps these ill-informed children have not been told of the vengeful witch that haunts their very own cemetery. Buried under a giant oak tree in Chesterville Cemetery are the restless remains of a murdered witch whose name has long been lost to time. Forever enclosed by an iron fence erected around her grave, the witch rises to seek revenge on those who ended her life.

- The large oak tree standing in the cemetery was planted over the witch's grave to prevent her from rising from the dead to seek her revenge. It is said that if the tree ever dies or is cut down, the spirit of the witch will forever be released.

- Many visitors to the cemetery have reported seeing the glowing ghost of the witch standing next to the tree that eternally traps her spirit.

History

Little is known about the actual history of the cemetery.

Several of the graves date back to the late 1880s. There are several older cemeteries in the area dating back to the 1830s and 1840s.

Investigation

The legend of the witch is widely known throughout the area.

One of the more popular stories states that many years ago a young woman in the Amish community began to question the teaching of the elders. As time passed, the woman began speaking out on the how unfairly women in the Amish community were perceived and treated. The strict elders were not pleased with her insubordination, so they started to spin a tale that evil forces were trying to penetrate the very soul of the community. As the woman became more vocal with her grievances, the elders quickly spread word that the woman had been doing the devil's bidding and was caught practicing witchcraft. Soon after that the woman simply vanished from

the community. A few days later her lifeless body was discovered in a field. The elders wanted to use her death as a warning to all those who questioned the faith. The body was put on display for anyone who was brave enough to visit. The body was also continuously watched by elders who feared the woman would rise from the dead to her seek justice. A short time later her body was laid to rest in the Chesterville Cemetery.

The cemetery is not an Amish cemetery. However, one person buried in the cemetery is a three-month-old girl named Harshbarger that died in 1874. Harshbarger is an Amish name.

Another version of the story states that the young woman was an accomplished healer that possessed supernatural powers that

allowed her to speak with animals. Fearful of her gifts, the woman was murdered for being a witch. In order to protect themselves from her angry spirit, the community planted a tree over her grave to prevent her spirit from rising. As an additional caution, a small iron fence was constructed around her grave to keep her spirit from roaming.

One day a visitor was walking around the cemetery when he reached his hand out for the trunk of the tree. As soon as his hand touched the tree, his body went cold as ice.

We spoke with a witness who was driving past the cemetery one evening when she spotted a transparent figure of a woman standing next to the witch's grave. Unfortunately, the witness did not stop to find out what the figure was doing there.

We were told that a woman went to visit the cemetery with her daughter. When they got out of their vehicle they were treated to the sounds of birds signing. As the mother approached the grave she was overcome with feelings of anger and loneliness. They felt they were being pushed away from the cemetery, and as they were about to leave, they noticed that the birds had stopped singing.

The Dare. At midnight, if you are brave enough to run into the cemetery and touch the tree, the spirit of the witch will make herself known to you.

Greenwood Cemetery

Location: Decatur, Macon County, Illinois
Address: 606 South Church Street, Decatur, IL 62522-3306

Directions: From W Decatur St. turn right on Church St. When Church St. comes to a T, follow it to the left and the cemetery will be straight ahead.

Ghost Lore

At first glance, Greenwood Cemetery looks like your everyday run of the mill graveyard. However, upon closer inspection you will certainly find that this cemetery is chalk full of legends and lore. From wandering Civil War spirits, to flooded ghosts searching for their home, this unique cemetery is far from anything normal.

- The cemetery is plagued with strange lights that hover and float throughout the grounds.

- Civil War soldiers continue to march and fight long after their days of combat are over.

History

1800s – No one is quite sure as to when the first burials took place on the hill. The first ten acres of land were purchased from David L. Allen for $60 an acre.

1838 – The first official burials took place on the hill. However, years before, numerous bodies from a different cemetery were dug up and transported to the cemetery to be re-buried.

1857 – Under poor management the cemetery was in shambles and it was considered a public disgrace. Reports of bodies being taken during nighttime grave robbing were common. Many of the local newspapers finally cried out for something to be done with the public eyesore.

1857 – Due to the unflattering condition of the cemetery, a group of concerned citizens heeded the call of the newspapers and decided to establish the Decatur Cemetery Association. The first point of business was to whip the Greenwood Cemetery into a more presentable condition.

1858 – At this point in time the cemetery was composed of only 40 acres of land. Later in the year, the Cemetery Association purchased an additional 36 acres of land.

1876 – Six more acres were purchased for the cemetery.

1893 – The official cemetery address was 726 South Greenwood Avenue.

1930-40s – For the second time, the cemetery fell into hard times. Many years of neglect had caused the cemetery to take on a rundown appearance. Cemetery board of trustees' president, J.A.Meriweather, believed that the erecting of the South Main gateway would attract more visitors.

1958 – The Decatur Township took over management and day-to-day operations of the cemetery. The first goal was to clean up the appearance of the cemetery and begin its preservation and restoration.

1967 – The official address of the cemetery was changed to its current address of 606 South Church Street.

Currently – There are over 30,000 people buried in the 100-acre cemetery. The Heritage Network of Decatur still gives walking tours of the cemetery.

Source: *History of Greenwood Cemetery* by Roy V. Terneus and the *Decatur Review.*

Investigation

The cemetery was not always the historic tour stop that it is today. In 1929, the *Decatur Evening Herald* reported that a group of

preachers who had done services in all the cemeteries in the county believed that Greenwood was the "worst they knew."

Years ago, the cemetery was damaged by a harsh flash flood that swept through the town. The southern portion of the cemetery was hardest hit. During the flooding, the rushing waters uprooted many graves. When the flood had subsided, workers were horrified to discover that many graves and skeletons had been washed away. Since that time, the southern portion of the graveyard has been home to reports of mysterious dancing balls of light. Local legend tells that the lights are the disembodied spirits of those flood victims who continue to search for their eternal rest. We were unable to find any written report of the flood.

Many tales of horror in the cemetery originated from the old mausoleum which sat inside the cemetery. Unfortunately the dilapidated mausoleum was torn down in 1967. Researcher Troy Taylor reported that when the mausoleum was standing it was a source for many strange events. Visitors reported hearing unearthly screams originating from the decrepit mausoleum. Others reported seeing mysterious lights that could never be accounted for. Although the

mausoleum is no longer physically standing, the area is still home to many reports of paranormal activity.

We spoke with a cemetery employee who informed us that the legend of the cemetery being haunted dated back many years. Although he was unsure as to whether he believed the cemetery was actually haunted, he did tell us that most of the eerie stories come from the Civil War section of the cemetery. Many unsuspecting visitors to the cemetery have been walking through the area when they catch a glimpse of a man roaming the cemetery. Yet, to their amazement, when they turn to get a closer look, the person is simply not there. Many researchers believe that these ghosts are the spirits of unfortunate Civil War soldiers who died and were buried while passing by the cemetery.

There may be a reason for the Civil War section to be haunted. An 1896 article from the *Decatur Republican* reported that cemetery caretaker R. J. Roberts was in charge of gathering as many of the names of the unknown fallen soldiers as he could. Roberts estimated that there were well over 200 unknown soldiers buried in the cemetery.

One-Armed Red of Lincoln Theater

Location: Decatur, Macon County, Illinois
Address: 141 North Main Street, Decatur, IL 62523-1206
Phone: (217) 422-1711

Directions: The theater is located right on Main St.

Ghost Lore

Throughout the U.S. many theaters have gained a haunted reputation. Many believe that those who participate in theater often do it for their love of performing, and when they pass away their spirits continue to try and entertain audiences just like when they were alive. Another theory states that the cast members and audience of theatres create a lot of emotional energy, and all that energy attracts lost spirits to the theatre. Yet, regardless of whether you believe the various theories, the Lincoln Theater is said to be haunted by a former stagehand by the name of Red, who continues to perform his duties even from the grave.

One evening Red was working up on the rafters of the theater when he lost his footing, slipped off the plank, and fell from the rafters. Red quickly began a downward spiral towards the ground when his arm got tangled in a few pulley ropes. His arm was ripped from its socket as the remainder of his bloody body crashed onto the stage below.

• Before the Lincoln Theater was built, the land housed a hotel. A tragic fire burned the hotel to the ground, and the charred remains of two guests were found smoldering in the rubble. Their spirits continue to inhabit the area.

• The ghostly image of a man has been spotted working inside the theater. When witnesses try to get a better look at the man, however, he simply disappears into thin air.

History

1915 – The Decatur & Arcade Hotel, which had occupied the land before the theater, burned down in a horrible fire that was responsible for at least two deaths and several missing persons.

1916 – The Lincoln Square Theater was constructed by Clarence Wait with a design by the architectural firm of Aschauer & Waggoner. Due to the rash of fires in the area the firm put in place many precautions in order to try to make the building fireproof.

1916 – The formal opening of the theater was held. The comedy *Hit the Trail Holiday* sold out and had overflowed with standing room only.

1926 – The theater hired a full orchestra to provide music for the shows.

1929 – The theater switched its focus from live theater and silent movies, and, like much of the country, began to show newer movies that had the benefit of sound.

1930s – The name of the theater was shortened when the Square was removed from it.

1936 – The original owner, Clarence Wait, passed away. Clarence's two brothers took over ownership of the theater.

1974 – The theater was sold to Plitt Theaters Inc.

1980 – The theater was shut down and sat empty.

1990s – By this time the theater was dilapidated and in desperate need of repair.

2001 – Carol Brinoette, the president of the Lincoln Square Board of Directors, announced the board's plans to raise funds for the theater.

2004 – The theater had received half of the $3.5 million that was pledged by the State of Illinois for renovation.

Source: *Decatur Herald and Review*

Investigation

Two lives were lost when the Decatur-Arcade Hotel burned down in 1915. Both W. E. Graham and C. S. Guild perished in the fire. Their deaths were covered by the local paper. On April 21, 1915, The *Decatur Daily Review* newspaper ran a feature article on the fire at the hotel. The headline read, "Screams of W. E. Graham heard by manager Hanthorn as flames enveloped him." Four days later, the paper ran this headline "Another Body in Ruins of Hotel?" The article reported that a search for the body of C. S. Guild was initiated. Guild, a 70-year-old traveling salesmen for a woolen mill in Jamestown, New York, who had stayed in the room directly under W. E. Graham, was said to be missing. Unfortunately Guild was not missing for long as on April 29th the paper reported that Guild's body had been found. The paper reported that a witness had reported hearing Guild's cries for help from within the raging fire. Mrs. Hue Singleton stated that, "I shall hear those cries as long as I live." Mrs. Singleton went on to say, "His voice carried above the noise of the flame and was filled with the terror he must have had when he knew himself lost in the corridor and doomed to die in the building."

As far as the validity of the stagehand story, researcher Troy Taylor found that there was indeed a stagehand named Red who worked at the theater during the 1920s. It is true that Red only had one arm, but he didn't lose it in a fall; he lost it in World War I. Taylor also found that Red did indeed die in the theater, yet instead of plunging to his death from above, Red simply fell asleep in the theater and did not wake up.

Visitors and staff report hearing the sounds of footsteps echoing throughout the theater, yet upon investigation no source for the phantom footsteps can be found. Footsteps are not the only strange noise reported in the theater, as others have reported hearing mysterious whispering and the sound of objects moving on their own.

We spoke with the Paranormal Activity Investigators who had investigated the theater. During their investigation, one of the members went back to the stage area in order to retrieve some additional equipment. While digging through her backpack, she noticed out of the corner of her eye, an older man standing next to the stage. The mysterious man dressed in a flannel shirt and overalls just stood there quietly watching her. Not knowing the identity of the man, the woman shined her flashlight on the area to catch a better view of him. However, she was too late, as the man had simply vanished. The woman was puzzled as to who this person was, as she did not hear him approach or leave.

Elkhart Cemetery

Location: Elkhart, Logan County, Illinois

Directions: Take N Gillett St. Follow the bend to the right, as it will turn into Chapel Rd., then into 700th St. Keep following this road and you will see the cemetery off to your right.

Ghost Lore

Losing someone close to you is one of the hardest challenges in life. People deal with the grief and sorrow in many different ways. One act that brings some solace to those mourning their loss is to visit their loved one's final resting place. With so many people visiting the cemetery plots of friends and family, it should not seem that odd when visitors report seeing the wife of Governor Oglesby visiting her husband's gravesite. However, what does seem odd to the witnesses is the fact that Gov. Oglesby's wife is also deceased and buried right next to him.

- Spirits of Native Americans have been seeing running through the cemetery and across the bridge that passes over the cemetery.

- In the back of the woods sits a warning sign that reads, "grounds keepers don't wander back here and neither should ladies and gents." If you do not head the warning, the sign will lead you off on a trail that you will not come back from.

History

1750 – The Illini Indians named the large hill of the area Elk Heart Hill, due the fact that they thought it resembled the shape of an elk's heart.

1763 – The Kickapoo (tribe from the Illini) Indians were settled on the hill with a small village.

1819 – James Latham, one of the first white men in the area, built his family a log cabin on the hill to farm and raise livestock.

1824 – Richard James Oglesby was born in Kentucky.

1860 – The village created the idea for Elkhart Cemetery, even though no land had yet been lotted and no system of burial was in place.

1865 – Oglesby was elected to be the governor of Illinois.

1866 – The village had the Elkhart Cemetery surveyed and lotted.

1873 – Governor Oglesby was re-elected as Illinois governor.

1885 – Once again Gov. Oglesby was re-elected by the people of Illinois.

1889 – Governor Oglesby retired and moved to Elkhart to spend time with his friends and family. He built a gigantic 41-room mansion in Elkhart dubbed "Oglehurst."

1899 – Governor Oglesby passed away in his home when he struck his head on a piece of furniture during a fall caused by vertigo. He was buried in the Elkhart Cemetery.

1984 – The Elkhart fire department set a controlled fire to Oglehurst.

Investigation

We spoke with several town residents who told us that for many years, townsfolk would whisper stories about the haunted cemetery and all of the strange legends that went with it. The chilling stories of the cemetery have been around for a long time.

We were told that those who go out to the cemetery at night often spot a woman paying her respect for the dead in front of Governor Oglesby's mausoleum. Thinking it is just another visitor to the popular cemetery, the witnesses really pay her no mind. However, once they get a bit closer to the mausoleum, they notice that the woman appears to be somewhat transparent. Intrigued by this, the

witnesses try to get even closer. As they move towards the mausoleum, the "woman" suddenly disappears right before their eyes. It is believed that this mourning woman is the wife of Gov. Olgesby who is coming back from the dead to visit him. However, since the governor was married twice during his life, we wonder which wife is actually visiting him.

Other residents told a different version of the tale. In this macabre version, the woman does not simply disappear from the mausoleum—she is chased off into the woods by a group of phantom Indians hellbent on capturing her. Many people have seen this strange chase take place and report that the wife always runs across the bridge near the cemetery to avoid capture and death.

Native American spirits have been spotted frequently in and around the cemetery. This does not come as a surprise, since the Native Americans were the first group of people to settle on the land and had many disputes and skirmishes with each other and with the pioneers while living on the land.

The Dare. In the back of the cemetery there is a trail that leads off into the woods. Local lore states that as you hike this trail it will split off into two other trails. If you make the crucial error of picking the wrong trail, you will disappear and never return. At the time of our investigation, there was no sign at the back of the cemetery warning visitors not to wander into the woods. The wooded trail does split off into many other trails. Luckily for us, we picked the right trails to hike, escaped death, and made it back safely.

Zion Cemetery

Location: Forest City, Mason County, Illinois

Directions: From Forest City, travel west towards Bishop for approximately 2.5 miles. There you will see a small Zion Cemetery sign and a large red barn. This small road will split, with the left route going to the barn and the right going to the cemetery.

Ghost Lore

The Zion Cemetery is nestled in a wooded area far enough from the main road to remain hidden from the prying eyes of passing motorists. Complete with vandalized headstones, odd pieces of litter, and empty beer cans, this place may seem like your run of the mill cemetery. However, what sets the place apart is that most people go to a cemetery after death, yet many of the people buried here actually met their death while at the cemetery. Let us explain the

37

story. Years ago, the Zion Church stood right next to the Zion Cemetery, and one day during church service the building mysteriously burst into flames. Many of the praying churchgoers inside met a fiery death. The charred bodies of the victims were buried right next door in the cemetery.

- The tormented spirits of those who tragically died in the fire continue to haunt the area.

- In the back of the cemetery is a gravestone that sits next to a large eerie tree. If you knock on the trunk of the tree, the spirit of the person buried beneath will scream at you.

- Mysterious noises often float throughout the cemetery. At night the sounds of young girls giggling can be heard coming from the dark woods surrounding the cemetery.

History

1841 – Mason County was established. The area was originally part of Tazewell County, which was formed in 1827.

1855 – The land was deeded to A. Himmel with the intent that it would be used for church purposes.

1885 – The cemetery land was platted by the Zion Church. It is believed that many people were buried on the land before it became an official cemetery.

1955 – The church building was removed from the deed of the property. Since the church building no longer existed, the fire had to have taken place before this date.

1976 – A permit was issued for a burial inside the cemetery. No more recent burials were located.

Investigation

The Zion Cemetery is sometimes referred to as Bishop Cemetery.

Long ago the Zion Church did sit on the land. One afternoon the church accidentally caught fire and burned to the ground.

According to local historians, the date of the fire has been lost to history, yet a 1955 report requests that the church building be removed from the deed making it the most likely time the fire occurred. It is also believed that the church was empty when it burned, and no one perished in the fire.

It appears that the story of the haunted cemetery has been circulating around the community for many years. A life-long resident of the area told us that 30 years ago, when he was a teenager, he would gather with his friends and dare one another to see who was brave enough to venture out to the haunted cemetery to see the ghosts.

Many of the townsfolk know of the haunted tales surrounding the cemetery. We spoke with a young woman who had gone out to the cemetery many times looking for the ghosts. While her friends all had strange things happen to them while at the cemetery, she did not have a personal experience.

It is believed that when you visit the cemetery, you will instantly feel an unusual cold breeze pass through your body. What fright-

ens visitors is the fact that this mysterious cold wind has been reported at all times of the year.

We were told that if you visit the cemetery at night and listen very closely, you can hear the sounds of phantom little girls giggling and playing in the surrounding woods. Numerous attempts to locate the source of the phantom giggling have failed.

The Dare. In the back of the cemetery buried next to a large tree is the grave where the former preacher of the church is buried. If you walk up to his grave and knock on the trunk of the tree, the noise of the knock will reverberate down through the roots into his casket. From his resting place beneath the tree, the preacher will let out an ear piercing shriek.

Park District Gym

Location: Havana, Mason County, Illinois
Address: 127 East Jefferson Street, Havana, IL 62644

Directions: From Main St., take Orange St. toward the Police Station. Turn right on Market St. Turn left on Pearl St. and the gym will be on your left.

Ghost Lore

Most people have a hard time getting to the gym. With the combination of family, friends, and hectic work schedules, many people simply don't have the time to frequent their gym. However, the Park District Gym has the opposite problem, because this gym can not get its members to leave, even after the member dies.

At the gym a young man had just finished a game of basketball and went downstairs to use the restroom. Somehow he became trapped or locked inside. Twenty-four hours later his dead body was found still trapped in the bathroom. It is believed that his ghost continues to haunt the gym looking for someone to play a game of basketball with.

- During the night visitors and staff have seen a ghostly apparition shooting a basketball in the gym.

- Mysterious noises have been reported throughout the building.

History

1923 – The gym was constructed.

2000 – The city purchased the gym from the school. The city also renovated the gym and removed the old boiler, added an upstairs restroom, and replaced the windows.

Currently – The basement of the gym is used for a workout facility, while the upstairs serves as venue for basketball games, dances, and other community events.

Investigation

We spoke with the current director of the gym who has worked at the building for over 10 years. Although she admits the place can be extremely creepy at night, she has not had a personal paranormal experience.

A staff member told us the story of one young man who got more than he bargained for when he was sent to complete his community service hours at the gym. The young man was working off his hours in the gym when he felt someone tap him on the shoulder. Spinning around to see who was there, the boy was terrified to find that no one was around. The young man was so spooked that he quickly darted for the exit. While trying to escape, the young man was suddenly hit in the face by an unexplained cold wind. The man was then convinced that something paranormal was taking place and ran for the door and flew outside and refused to ever return to the gym. After hearing about the man running off, the gym's director spoke with him to get the details. The director thought that the young man was truly scared by what took place in the gym.

A woman told us that she often gets an eerie feeling at night while working alone in the building. She said that it feels as though you are not alone and that some other presence is also inside the building.

The director informed us that, to her knowledge, no one has ever died in the downstairs men's restroom. We were unable to verify the story that a man died in the basement.

The lore of the gym's haunted reputation is well-known within the community.

Campground Cemetery

Location: Mattoon, Coles County, Illinois
AKA: The Old Sawyer Cemetery

Directions: From 45 take Lake Paradise Rd. (400N) to the south for approximately two miles. You will run into Lake Rd. (250E) turn left and the cemetery will be directly on your right.

Ghost Lore

The town of Mattoon is well known around the country as the home of the Mad Gasser. In the 1940s, the small town was plagued by a phantom anesthetist that orchestrated a series of gas attacks on townsfolk. The town of Mattoon has undergone significant changes in the past 70 years, yet one thing that remains the same is the abundance of paranormal activity. Silently resting on old church grounds is the Campground Cemetery. Here on what was known as God's acre, worshippers are so devout that not even death can prevent them from celebrating their faith.

Years ago, the cemetery was a campground for thousands of worshippers that attended the outdoor services.

- Picnickers dressed in Victorian-age clothing have been spotted inside the cemetery.
- The spirit of a nun has been spotted floating through the graveyard.
- The Sheriff's Department is often notified of vandals in the cemetery, yet when they go to the cemetery to investigate, they find it completely empty.

History

1828 – The Wabash Point Methodist Society was established.

1834 – Along the banks of the Little Wabash River, worshippers constructed a small primitive Methodist Episcopal church to be used for services.

1830s-50s – The area was used as a campground for those traveling from across the region to worship at the site. The services were so popular that thousands of visitors would set up camp in order to avoid missing one single service.

1854 – The first official funeral ceremony was held for Willis H. Clark.

2003 – Vandals broke and destroyed numerous stones in the cemetery.

Investigation

In the 1800s, thousands of worshippers would descend on the area to participate in religious services. Each year several people would pass away during the festivities. The deceased needed a proper burial, and so to accommodate the families of the dead, a few graves were plotted in a piece of adjoining land. The unofficial cemetery was called "God's Acre." It didn't take long for other members of the surrounding communities to bring their dead to the newly formed cemetery as well. Years later, in paying homage to the history of the area, the cemetery's name was changed to Campground Cemetery.

We spoke with a woman who recalled camping near the cemetery while she was a Girl Scout. During weekend camping trips, the girls would gather around the fire and listen to the troop leader tell ghostly stories of spirits haunting the cemetery. The main ghost haunting the cemetery was said to be the spirit of Sister Mary Worth.

One young man was passing by the cemetery when he thought he spotted several people enjoying a picnic inside the cemetery. What struck the man odd was the fact that the picnickers dressed and looked like they were from the 1800s. When the man looked back at the cemetery to get a better view, the images were gone.

In 2003, the *Mattoon Journal Gazette* reported that vandals broke many gravestones in the cemetery. Stone-setting specialists Kevin Baumann and Justin Clark tried to repair much of the damage. We also spoke with the Coles County Sheriff's Department. They did confirm that they have received calls of vandals in the cemetery.

Train Bridge

Location: Rushville, Schuyler County, Illinois

Directions: From Rushville take Hwy 24 north. Turn right on Timothy (LN 125 E). After approximately 1.5 miles the road turns to gravel. Take your 1st right onto 1460 N (Sugar CR Bottom Rd.), the bridge will be straight ahead.

Ghost Lore

There is an old train bridge located far out in the county where many unexplained events have taken place. The secluded bridge is haunted by several ghosts who were murdered on the bridge, and at night phantom trains have been seen, heard, and felt steaming their way towards the bridge, yet no train ever comes.

A horrible accident took place when a train crashed into a school bus full of children, killing everybody on board.

- At night eerie screams from some mysterious entity have been heard.

- Oftentimes the sounds of trees falling will be heard under the train bridge.

History

We were unable to locate any history of the bridge. Most of the town had never heard of the bridge. Interviews with the newspaper, library, and local historians turned up nothing on the bridge.

Investigation

The old wooden train bridge overlooking the railroad tracks is said to be home for many paranormal events. It is here that curious travelers set out to experience something out of the ordinary.

One of the more popular stories of the bridge revolves around the phantom trains. A young man shared with us his personal experi-

ence, as one night he was out at the bridge with a few friends waiting for something to happen. Soon after they got there they heard the sound of a cat crying. At the same time as the cat noise, the bridge started to move and shake beneath their feet. The group forgot about the "cat" and quickly looked for the oncoming train. Much to their surprise, they could see no train, yet the shaking of the bridge became more intense. Convinced that a train was coming, the confused group again looked down at the track only to discover empty darkness. A few seconds later the bridge stopped shaking, and the frightened group quickly left the area.

Another local tale about the bridge involves a school bus that was transporting children to school one morning when it collided with an oncoming train, killing all of the kids on board. Because of this accident, when you go to the bridge at night you can see the ghosts of the spirits of the kids roaming the area where they met their fate.

We spoke with a man who told us that many years ago he was out at the bridge when he heard the sounds of several children crying. Thinking he was imagining the noise, the man asked his friend to

also listen for the sound. Together they both heard the faint cry of children coming from somewhere in the darkness.

Another version of the crying voices legend comes from the story of a train that was passing through town. As the steamer passed over the bridge, it hit an object that had been left on the tracks by some local pranksters. This prank caused the train to derail and crash, resulting in the untimely deaths of everyone on board. It is believed that the spirits of the people killed in the crash are forever haunting the bridge, looking to seek revenge on pranksters who cost them their lives.

We were unable to locate any story of a train crashing or derailing at the bridge.

The Dare. Many of the residents told us that if you go out to the track at midnight, you will come face to face with a phantom train.

Lincoln's Home

Location: Springfield, Sangamon County, Illinois
Address: 426 South Seventh Street, Springfield, IL 62701-1901
Phone: (217) 492-4241, ext. 221

Ghost Lore

Most people are familiar with the story of Abraham Lincoln being born in a tiny one-room log cabin in Kentucky, complete without running water or electricity. The lasting image of Lincoln in a log cabin is quickly shattered when visitors travel to his Springfield home. Here, instead of finding an old run down cabin, visitors are shocked to find that Lincoln lived in an elegant, spacious, and fur-niture-filled home. Visitors are also surprised to find out that, although no one lives in the house, it is by no means empty.

History

1839 – On the corner of Eighth and Jackson Streets, the cozy one-and-a-half story cottage was constructed.

1842 – Abraham Lincoln and Mary Todd were married.

1843 – Abraham and Mary rented the home.

1844 – Soon after the birth of his son Robert, Lincoln purchased the Eighth Street home.

1850 – Tragedy hit the Lincolns where their second son Eddie died shortly before his fourth birthday.

1851 – The Lincolns celebrated the birth of another boy they named William.

1853 – The final Lincoln child was born. The Lincolns named him Thomas.

1856 – Feeling cramped due to several new additions to the family, the Lincolns added a full second story to their home.

1860 – The family moved to Washington, D.C. The family struggled to decide whether they should sell the home or just rent it out while they were away. Memories and nostalgia finally won out and the home was rented out.

1865 – After the death of the President, Mary Todd felt she could not return to the home where so many wonderful memories of her husband lingered, and the home continued to be rented out.

1865 – Immediately after his death, visitors started to flock to Springfield to get a glimpse of the President's home.

1887 – Robert Lincoln donated the home to the State of Illinois.

1906 – A large elm tree that was said to have been planted by Lincoln himself was destroyed in a storm.

1931 – President Herbert Hoover, while in town for the tomb dedication, could not pass up the opportunity to visit the Lincoln home.

1950 – Preserving the home was brought to the forefront, when, in order to help control the temperature and humidity in the home, window fans were installed.

1972 – The home was donated to the United States of America. It was to be the job of the National Park Service to protect and preserve the historic home.

1987 – The home was closed for major renovations and a plastic shell was constructed over the home for protection.

1988 – The newly renovated home re-opened.

Currently – The home is open to the public through free tours that take place daily.

Source: National Park Service

Investigation

It is believed that the spirits haunting the Lincoln home are those of Abraham Lincoln, his wife Mary, and several former servants.

A 1976 article in the *State Journal Register* reported that a housekeeper named Shirlee Laughlin believed the house was haunted. One day while rearranging the furniture in Mary's room, she paused for a moment trying to decide whether the small chair in front of her would look better in a different room. While contemplating the move, Shirlee was touched on the shoulder by someone or something. When she turned to see who had grabbed her shoulder, she discovered that she was alone. Shirlee said that she "left the chair right where it was."

The *State Journal Register* also reported that Lincoln's ghost often is sighted moving through the home where he once lived. Lincoln's old rocking chair has been seen slowly rocking back and forth, creaking under the weight of some unseen specter.

We spoke with a park guide who told us that the official National Park Service stance was that ghosts do not exist. However, not speaking for the Park Service, he told us that many employees have witnessed some odd occurrences while inside the home. In addition to the rocking chair, employees have heard the hushed whispers of people talking in the home, although no source for the mysterious noises have even been found.

Other employees spoke with us, stating that a number of times after a tour of the home is completed, visitors will approach them to ask if the home is rumored to have any ghosts. When told about the lore surrounding the home, the visitor will state that while on the tour, they could have sworn that they saw a shadowy figure of someone moving through the house, yet when they turned to get a better look, the image had disappeared.

If Lincoln is indeed rising from the dead to visit the site of his old home, he seems to be even busier in death than he was in life, as nearly every area of Springfield has been home to a sighting of his wandering spirit.

Lincoln's Tomb

Location: Springfield, Sangamon County, Illinois
Address: Oak Ridge Cemetery, 1500 Monument Avenue,
Springfield, IL 62702-2500

Directions: From N Grand Ave. W, turn on Monument Dr. and
arrive at the tomb. There are direction signs all over the area.

Ghost Lore

Abraham Lincoln served as the 16th President of the Untied States.
Those who knew him often spoke highly of his intellect, passion,
honesty, and integrity. These admirable traits have helped him
become a sort of superhero of history. He is universally regarded
as one of the greatest leaders in U.S. history, his portrait graces the
U.S. penny and five dollar bill, his stoic face anchors Mt.
Rushmore, and his enduring memory continues to live on in the
hearts and minds of millions of people. However, visitors to the
Lincoln Tomb believe that it is more than his memory that lives on.

- For many years the spectral image of Lincoln has been spotting wandering around the crypt.

- The sounds of phantom footsteps pacing the halls have echoed through the tomb's corridors throughout the years.

- The soft sounds of weeping mourners can be heard in the empty building.

Millions of visitors have traveled to the tomb to pay their respects to the fallen President. However, little do they know the tomb does not contain Lincoln's remains.

History

1865 – The first funeral service was held for the President at the White House.

1865 – The National Lincoln Monument Association was created to plan for the construction of Lincoln's Tomb. Illinois Governor

Richard Oglesby headed the group of men that also included many of the President's friends and colleagues.

1865 – The remains of Lincoln were placed on a special train for the 1,700 mile ride to Springfield. Also on the train were the remains of Lincoln's son, William (Willie). The train stopped for ten more funeral services before it pulled into Springfield.

1868 – The Monument Association chose sculptor Larkin Mead's design for the tomb.

1869 – Construction of a tomb for Lincoln was started. The cost of the project was estimated to cost $171,000.

1874 – Nearly ten years after his demise, the dedication ceremony was held for Lincoln's tomb.

1876 – An attempt was made to steal the body of Lincoln. Luckily, the body was recovered.

1895 – Richard Oglesby, who was the only surviving member of the Monument Association, deeded the property to the State of Illinois.

1900 – The old tomb was torn down and a new tomb was created for Lincoln. His body was to be surrounded by 20 inches of concrete to ward off any further attempts to steal his body.

1901 – A large crowd gathered to witness the final burial of Lincoln.

1960 – The tomb was designated a National Historic Landmark.

1966 – The tomb was placed on the National Register of Historic Places.

Source: Illinois Historic Preservation Agency

Investigation

Lincoln's 117-foot tomb was constructed using brick that was encased with Quincy granite. The entrance is to the tomb is decorated with a bronze replication of the marble head of Lincoln that was created by Gutzon Borglum (the sculptor of Mt. Rushmore). The interior halls of the tomb are covered with shined marble trimmed in bronze. Statues of Lincoln, along with plaques containing excerpts of some of his most memorable speeches, adorn the tomb's hallways.

Since the time Lincoln's body was placed to rest in Springfield, stories of his restless soul wandering the crypt have been told and retold. Witnesses have reported seeing the ghostly figure of Lincoln leisurely walking about the area. What strikes the witnesses as

being odd is the fact that he looks as though he is deep in thought and oblivious to his surroundings.

We spoke with a long time staff member of the tomb regarding the strange ghostly lore that has formed around the tomb. Although he had yet to have any first-hand experiences, he knew of many fellow workers who were not so unlucky. He told us that often times, after a bustling day full of curious visitors, the staff would lock up the doors and begin their daily maintenance of the tomb. While working, the staff would hear the sounds of soft cries coming from the tomb. Thinking that a few mourners had not finished paying their respects, the staff would make their way to the tomb to notify the visitors that the tomb was now closed. However, every time they reached the tomb, the area was completely empty and the mysterious crying had suddenly stopped.

Inside the chambers of the tomb, the puzzling sounds of someone pacing back and forth across the floor can be heard. These phantom footsteps have never been traced to any living source. Most believe the origin of the continuous pacing can be attributed to the restless spirit of Lincoln which refuses to remain in the tomb.

The tomb of Lincoln does not have the exclusive rights to his ghost, as the wandering spirit of Lincoln has been detected in numerous locations throughout Springfield, including the president's former home.

Most historians discredit the idea that Lincoln's body is not buried in the tomb. Since the moment Lincoln's casket arrived in Springfield, rumors of the missing body have been circulating. The timeless legend seems to have started in part by the constant moving and hiding of Lincoln's body. Of course, the official reason for the secrecy was so that the body would stay hidden from the reaches of unsavory burglars looking to snatch up the presidents remains. In 1901, several witnesses were present when Lincoln's casket was once again opened up and inspected. Upon inspection, the group was able to verify that a body was indeed in the casket, and that the body was that of Abraham Lincoln.

Turning Angel of Calvary Cemetery

Location: Springfield, Sangamon County, Illinois

Directions: From Monument Rd. (road to Lincoln's tomb), turn right on Eastman Ave. Turn left on 3rd St. From there, turn onto Black St. and the cemetery will be on your left. The angel is located directly across the street from the cemetery office building, right along the fence.

Ghost Lore

Many years ago, a young man in town named Carl was severely distraught over the death of his lovely wife Louisa. Overcome with grief, Carl decided that he needed to forever honor his lost wife's memory. Carl purchased a statue of a beautiful angel that was positioned on top of his wife's gravestone. The angel statue was meant to represent the beauty and purity of his wife's soul. A few years later, Carl joined his wife in the family burial plot. The memory of the undying love Carl had for his wife has long since been forgotten to time. The only reminder is the angel monument that rests on their gravestone. Well, "rests" is certainly not the best way to describe the angel that sits on the family grave, as many late night visitors to the grave claim that the angel statue will actually move right before your eyes.

- At midnight those courageous souls that risk entering the cemetery will see the statue of the angel move on its own.

- A mournful weeping is often heard coming directly from the angel statue.

History

1857 – Because the members of the Church of St. John had no place to bury their dead, 16 acres of land adjoining the Oak Ridge Cemetery were purchased to serve as a cemetery.

1860 – The first burials in the cemetery took place.

1890 – Members of SS. Peter and Paul's and Sacred Heart formed an association which would be charged with the job of caring for the cemetery.

1891 – Due to the popularity of the cemetery, several additional lots were purchased and the cemetery consisted of 40 acres.

1906 – In order to qualify for bequests and endowments, the cemetery association was incorporated under the name "German Catholic Cemetery Association, Springfield, Illinois."

1922 – The association purchased an additional 24 acres of land north of the old cemetery grounds.

1924 – With the addition of the old cemetery lands, the association

declared that the cemetery would be named Calvary Cemetery.

1950 – The *Illinois State Register* reported that cemetery land was dedicated as the American Legion burial plot. The main speaker of the service was Rev. James J. Haggerty.

1965 – The Sheriff's deputies reported that nearly 20 gravestones were toppled by vandals. Many other stones were also damaged at a cost of several hundred dollars.

1975 – The Sheriff's Department was once again called to the cemetery when a youth discovered a skull lying on the ground. Authorities believed that the find was that of a very old human skull. Animals were listed as the possible cause of the skull being dug up.

Investigation

The angel statue sits on top of the grave marking the Mohay family. Buried in the family plots are the remains of Carl, Louisa, Therisa, and Rosa Mohay. Carl died in 1903, just days after his first birthday. Louisa passed away in 1908, at the age of four years and two months. Obviously, the story of Carl and Louisa being husband and wife is untrue. A much more plausible story is told by cemetery officials. Based on their records, the angel stature was constructed as a memorial to the deceased Mohay children.

We were able to track the legend of the turning angel in Calvary Cemetery back to the 1940s. It is possible that the legend dates all the way back to the death of Lousia in 1908.

In 1987, the *Illinois State Journal* reported that the statue has been a victim of vandals. Throughout the years, people have repeatedly broken pieces from the statue, including the arms and fingers. The paper also reported that at one point the cemetery had to hire its own security officers to keep out curious nighttime visitors.

The cemetery staff told us that each year hundreds of curious legend seekers visit the grave hoping to encounter the spirit of the turning angel.

We spoke with a young man who ventured out to the cemetery with a group of friends to see if the legend was true. On the drive to the cemetery, the group talked tough about what they would do if the legend ended up being true. The young man said the excitement and anticipation of getting to the cemetery created an air of electricity within the group. Once the group got to the cemetery, the energy quickly dissipated. It seemed talking about what they were going to do was much easier than actually doing it. After a few minutes, the group got the collective courage to walk to the angel statue. While he was there, the young man was certain that the statue did not move, yet several of his friends ran off to the car screaming that the statue had moved right before their eyes. To this day, the witnesses are convinced that the story of the turning angel is true.

The Dare. If you enter the cemetery during the witching hour of midnight and stand by the grave, you will see the angel move on its own.

Effland Woods

Location: Vermont, Fulton County, Illinois

Directions: Take Main St. out of town. It becomes Cty. Rd. 13.
Turn left on Quarter Rd. and follow for approximately 1 mile.
You will see a road (E2400) that turns to your right. The
woods will be on your left.

Ghost Lore

For years people have feared what lies within the dark enchanted
forests of the U.S. Many books and movies are based on stories
that use the woods to play on our fears of the dark and the
unknown. Often these woods are filled with ghosts, monsters, and
creepy mysteries. Yet, these things only exist in movies, right?
Well, not to those who visit the place locals call Effland Woods.
Years ago it is said that a small dirt road ran through the old woods,
providing a convenient path for travelers to get to town.

Unfortunately tragedy hit, and several people were killed in an accident on the road. Even though the road has since been swallowed up from plain sight, those who died on the road forever haunt the area where their life was taken from them.

- Unexplained colored balls of light can be seen hovering and moving through the woods during dark nights.

- Strange whistling noises and the eerie sounds of someone talking follow those who walk through the woods.

History

The area of woods is called the Effland Woods after the family that once owned and farmed the land.

The Effland family has not lived in the area for over 40 years.

Investigation

The correct name of the wooded land is Effland and not "Elfins," as many websites and people erroneously call it. The farmhouse where the Effland family once lived was just up the road from where the woods are.

The place is currently a dense forest, and several residents were unaware of any roads back in the woods. They stated that if roads through the woods were once used it was many years ago. Others in the area told us that the remains of the dirt road is still hidden in the woods, but it is not currently passable.

A woman from the area informed us that, although she did not know of any deaths that took place in the woods, the area is certainly "a large, dense, creepy place."

We spoke with a woman who told us that her son went out into the woods to hunt raccoon. She wished him good luck and sent him off on his hunt. About an hour later, the woman was surprised to see

that her son had came home early. The son looked like he was in a state of shock. Curious as to what had happened, the woman asked her son why he was back so early from his hunt. The son was pretty shaken up and never told his mother what happened to him while he was out hunting. The only thing he ever said about his experience was that he would never go hunting in those woods again.

On dark evenings while traveling the old country road, several passersby have looked into the woods and spotted strange balls of lights floating through the trees. Many of the witnesses were too frightened to get out of their cars to investigate the strange lights, preferring to stay in their car until they were in the safety of their home.

CHICAGO
ILLINOIS

Biograph Theater

Location: Chicago, Cook County, Illinois
Official Name: Victory Gardens Biograph Theater
Address: 2433 North Lincoln Avenue, Chicago, IL 60614-2414
Phone: (773) 348-4123 or (773) 549-5788
Box Office Phone: (773) 871-3000 (Tuesday-Saturday, 12 pm to 8 pm, Sunday 12 pm to 4 pm
TTY: (773) 871-0682
Email: tickets@victorygardens.org or information@victorygardens.org
Website: www.victorygardens.org

Ghost Lore

John Dillinger. The name alone still arouses curiosity and fanfare. He was considered the original public enemy #1 and is arguably the most notorious criminal of all time even 80 years after his death. Dillinger's lore penetrated the national curiosity, and he was known throughout the world as a suave bank robber who possessed an uncanny ability to outsmart the authorities. Even when the police finally captured him, he simply broke himself out of prison with a fake gun. The legend of John Dillinger grew each time the newspapers printed daily stories of his heroic escapes from the law.

What was so special about John Dillinger? Famous criminals had been around for quite a while. Al Capone, Lucky Luciano, and others that came before him were certainly just as well-known to the public, yet none of his predecessors rose to the level of fame that Dillinger did. The reason that Dillinger captured the nation's imagination was that he possessed one attribute that all the others lacked. Simply put, John Dillinger was extremely well-liked by the majority of the U.S. population. In some circles, he was even looked upon as a hero.

Yet even his fame and popularity could not stop Dillinger's luck from running out. After several years of fabulous escapes and amazing luck, Dillinger was finally brought down by the betrayal of a woman. Or was he?

- Cold spots.

- Feelings of trepidation.

- Apparitions of John Dillinger.

History

1903 – John Herbert Dillinger was born in Indianapolis, Indiana. He was born to a grocer named John Wilson Dillinger.

1914 – The theater was constructed by architect Samuel N. Crowen.

1920s – The building was owned by Henry Ericsson.

1922 – A holding company purchased the theater.

1934 – Dillinger and his gang were involved in an infamous shootout in Wisconsin that left one civilian and one law enforcement officer dead.

1934 – John Dillinger was gunned down outside the theater as he tried to escape the authorities by running down the alley.

1974 – The theater was sold to a land trust. It was planned to be demolished to be used as a parking lot.

2001 – The site was designated a Chicago Landmark.

2002 – The theater was running under the Village Theatres chain.

2004 – The theater was shut down again.

2004 – The Victory Gardens Theater announced their purchase of the theater. Their goal was to re-open the building as a live venue theater. Architect Daniel Coffey was in charge of the transformation.

2006 – Victory Gardens opened the newly renovated 299-seat theater to the public.

Investigation

First and foremost, this case is based on the assumption that Dillinger did indeed die in the alleyway outside the Biograph Theater on July 22, 1934. Author Jay Robert Nash was the first mainstream author to claim that the man gunned down at the Biograph was not John Dillinger. Nash postulates that the person who died outside the theater was a petty criminal from Wisconsin named Jimmy Lawrence who was set up to take the heat off of Dillinger. Nash lists strange irregularities with the body, including that the victim's eyes were brown while Dillinger's were gray, and that the body showed marks and illnesses that Dillinger did not have. Furthermore, Dillinger's own father stated that the body was not that of his son, On the other hand, most Dillinger scholars believe that it was indeed Dillinger that died that fateful evening. What is the truth? Well, you make up your own mind.

On July 22, 1934 Dillinger was at the Biograph enjoying a movie with his girlfriend and her friend, Anna Sage. Dillinger had no idea that Sage had brought him there to meet his fate. Sage had notified the authorities that she would bring Dillinger to the theater. For them to identify her, she would wear a red dress. After the show, the unsuspecting Dillinger walked out and just as he passed the alleyway Melvin Purvis and his men started shooting at him. Dillinger had no chance of escape and was hit with several bullets then fell to the ground dead in the alley. Immediately, the town was abuzz with the gossip of the death of Dillinger and hundreds of curiosity seekers crowded the alleyway. Some even dipped their scarves or handkerchiefs into Dillinger's blood for a souvenir.

The paranormal activity of this case is reported in both the historic theater and in the alleyway where Dillinger took his last breath.

Throughout the years, numerous people have reported seeing the ghostly image of a man running through the alleyway near the theater. The first thing that witnesses notice is the man's peculiar clothing. They report that he is dressed like he is from the early 1900s. It is believed that the ghost is that of Dillinger running down the alley where he drew his last breath.

Inside the theater, many staff and visitors have reported strange

activity. The most common phenomenon is an apparition of a man who is spotted moving throughout the building. Although the witnesses only catch a glimpse of the passing spirit, they are convinced it is the restless ghost of John Dillinger.

Other patrons of the theater have been inside enjoying the entertainment when out of nowhere they are suddenly overcome with a bone freezing chill. The source of this mysterious roaming cold spot has never been discovered.

It appeared to us that the new company is less than pleased with the theater's past and it is likely they will do little to promote it. We spoke with several employees of Victory Gardens who told us that after they moved into the building they had heard stories of the strange activity taking place; however, they did not have any new information to add.

The Biograph Theater alleyway is not the only place in the U.S. that claims the ghost of John Dillinger. The Little Bohemia Restaurant located in the small town of Manitowish Waters in northern Wisconsin is also rumored to have the spirit of Dillinger roaming the property. Little Bohemia is the place where Dillinger and his gang barely escaped a nasty shootout with the authorities who botched yet another attempt to catch Dillinger.

The Devil Baby

Location: Chicago, Cook County, Illinois
Address: Jane Addams Hull-House Museum, 800 South
Halsted Street, Chicago, IL 60607-4400
Phone: (312) 413-5353
Fax: (312) 413-2092
Hours: Tuesday - Friday 10 am to 4 pm Sunday noon to 4
pm. Closed Mondays and Saturdays.
Admission: Free
E-mail: jahh@uic.edu
Website: www.hullhousemuseum.org

Ghost Lore

In 1968, Roman Polanski made the film *Rosemary's Baby*, and it
scared the bejesus out of a lot of people. It was based on the novel
by Ira Levin about a young woman—impregnated by Lucifer himself—who gives birth to a "devil baby." It is said that the inspira-

tion for Levin's book came from a real-life event that happened in Chicago. Stories have circulated for many years that the Jane Addams Hull-House, said to be haunted, once harbored a Devil Baby that was hidden away in the attic.

- The house is haunted by Mrs. Hull. People claim to have heard her footsteps, felt her presence, and seen her apparition.

- People have seen the ghastly face of the devil child gazing out from an upstairs window.

- Hooded monks have been sighted.

- People have reported hearing "strange and unearthly noises."

Note. The museum is open for tours, but they don't allow you to take pictures inside, and they won't allow you to go upstairs. The curators deny the house is haunted and dismiss the stories of the devil baby. We recommend you take one of the ghost tours that bring you there after dark.

History

1856 – Hull-House was constructed by Charles Jerrold Hull (1820-1889).

1860 – Jane Addams was born in Cedarville, IL.

1880s – Hull-House went through several changes. It was used as a second-hand furniture store, a home for the elderly run by Little Sisters of the Poor, and later the lower part of it was used for offices and storerooms for a factory that stood behind it.

1889 – Hull granted the house to his niece who in turn granted it to Jane Addams. It was there that Addams and her college friend, Ellen Starr Gates, founded the social settlement Hull-House. The house was a shelter for women and for the homeless.

1931 – Jane Addams was awarded the Nobel Peace Prize.

1935 – Addams died and was buried in her hometown of Cedarville, IL.

1963 – Hull-House was purchased by the University of Illinois-Circle Campus.

1967 – The building was renovated by Frazier, Raftery, Orr, and Fairbank.

Investigation

The Hull-House is considered by many to be the most haunted house in all of Chicago.

The Ghost. The wife of Charles Hull died of natural causes in one of the upstairs bedrooms. Shortly after her death, overnight guests reported hearing footsteps in the very room in which she passed away.

When the house was occupied by the Little Sisters of the Poor, the residents believed the attic was haunted. Those who slept on the second floor blocked the stairs to the attic with a pitcher of water because of their belief that ghosts were unable to cross moving water.

When Jane Addams moved into the house, she slept in Mrs. Hull's bedroom and would be awakened at night to the sound of footsteps. She promptly moved to a different room. Ellen Gates and several

others also heard the footsteps. Author Helen Stuart Campbell (1839-1918) was challenged to spend the night in the room. She woke up to find an apparition standing at the foot of her bed. The figure disappeared as soon as a light was turned on.

The Devil Baby. In 1913, rumors began to circulate that Jane Addams was harboring a "Devil Baby" at Hull-House. People came by the hundreds—some even offering to pay admission—just to catch a glimpse of this monstrous child. the curious were consistently turned away at the door because Addams and the staff denied the veracity of the stories.

According to the Italian version of the story, a devout Catholic woman married a staunch atheist. When she put a picture of the Virgin Mary on her wall, he tore it down and smashed it, exclaiming he would rather have the Devil living in his house than to have that picture on the wall. Shortly thereafter, the young woman became pregnant and gave birth to a deformed child with scale-covered skin, cloven hooves for feet, pointed ears, horns on its head, and a small tail. It was said the child could walk and talk at birth, liked to smoke cigars, and would use obscene language. The

parents believed the satanic-looking child was a punishment for the father's remark. The horrified parents placed the baby in Hull-House in the care of Jane Addams. When the staff members brought the child to a priest to have it baptized, it resisted—leaping out of their arms and running across the pews. Later, it was seen laughing and dancing. The child was subsequently kept locked away in the attic of Hull-House where it later died.

Another version of the story claims a pregnant Jewish mother with six daughters was hoping to finally have a son. Her husband made the thoughtless comment that he would rather she give birth to the Devil himself than to another girl. This remark resulted in the birth of the Devil Baby.

In her autobiography, Jane Addams attempted to debunk the stories of the Devil Baby, but she insisted the reports of hearing footsteps and seeing apparitions in the upper rooms were absolutely true.

Chicago ghost tours visit the Hull-House at night. Many people report seeing the fiendish face of the Devil Baby peering out from the attic window. Several tourists have taken photos through the windows of the house and captured images of apparitions. Frequently, people can see the apparition of a woman in the LCD display on their digital cameras and actually watch her as she ascends the staircase.

Although the museum downplays the Devil Child legend, if asked, the staff will tell some of the history of the story with a skeptical tone in their voices.

Eastland Disaster

Location: Chicago, Cook County, Illinois
Address: Southeast corner of LaSalle Street and Wacker Drive

Ghost Lore

Most everyone has heard of the sinking of the Titanic, but few have heard of the Eastland Disaster in which 845 men, women and children perished in the Chicago River. It was the worst maritime accident to occur in the continental United States during the 20th century and the third worst ship disaster ever. Although the tragedy has been largely forgotten, restless spirits seem to call out from the murky waters demanding to be remembered.

- Ghostly sounds of crying, moaning, and screaming have been heard.

- Faces and shadowy apparitions have been seen beneath the surface of the water.

History

1902 – The passenger ship S.S. Eastland was built by the Jenks Ship Building Company after being commissioned by the Michigan Steamship Company.

1906 – The Chicago-South Haven Line purchased the ship.

1914 – It was sold to the St. Joseph-Chicago Steamship Company.

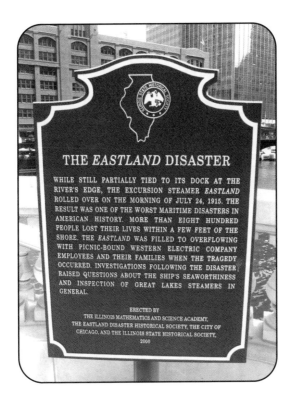

THE *EASTLAND* DISASTER

WHILE STILL PARTIALLY TIED TO ITS DOCK AT THE RIVER'S EDGE, THE EXCURSION STEAMER *EASTLAND* ROLLED OVER ON THE MORNING OF JULY 24, 1915. THE RESULT WAS ONE OF THE WORST MARITIME DISASTERS IN AMERICAN HISTORY. MORE THAN EIGHT HUNDRED PEOPLE LOST THEIR LIVES WITHIN A FEW FEET OF THE SHORE. THE *EASTLAND* WAS FILLED TO OVERFLOWING WITH PICNIC-BOUND WESTERN ELECTRIC COMPANY EMPLOYEES AND THEIR FAMILIES WHEN THE TRAGEDY OCCURRED. INVESTIGATIONS FOLLOWING THE DISASTER RAISED QUESTIONS ABOUT THE SHIP'S SEAWORTHINESS AND INSPECTION OF GREAT LAKES STEAMERS IN GENERAL.

ERECTED BY
THE ILLINOIS MATHEMATICS AND SCIENCE ACADEMY,
THE EASTLAND DISASTER HISTORICAL SOCIETY, THE CITY OF
CHICAGO, AND THE ILLINOIS STATE HISTORICAL SOCIETY,
2000

1915 – July 24. The Eastland Disaster. The ship capsized in the Chicago River. In October, it was raised.

1918 – The Eastland was sold to the Illinois Naval Reserve and recommissioned as the USS Wilmette. It was refitted as a naval training vessel and used during WWI and WWII.

1945 – The Eastland was decommissioned.

1946 – The ship was sold to the Hyman Michaels Co. for scrap.

1947 – The Eastland was demolished.

Investigation

On July 24, 1915, the Western Electric Company hired the S.S. Eastland to transport their employees to the annual company picnic in Michigan City, Indiana. The ship was moored to the dock between LaSalle and Clark Streets on the south bank of the Chicago River. As the passengers boarded, the ship began to keel

over. When the crew attempted to balance the ship by adjusting the ballast tanks, they over-adjusted, and the Eastland capsized. Because of the inclement weather that day, many of the passengers were below the deck and became trapped in. They either drowned or were crushed by heavy furniture. Sadly, of the 2,572 passengers on board, 845 people died in the tragedy, including 22 entire families. It was Chicago's worst single disaster. After hauling up dozens of dead bodies, one of the rescue divers went insane and had to be restrained.

Many of the recovered bodies were put in Chicago's Second Regiment Armory which currently houses Oprah's Harpo Studios. Hundreds of citizens had the gruesome task of filing past the corpses to identify dead friends and family members.

A historical plaque commemorates the disaster. Passersby and tourists visiting the site have reported hearing ghostly sounds and seeing faces and figures in the water as if the river retains the memories of the suffering and terror of that tragic day.

Haunted Harpo Studios

Location: Chicago, Cook County, Illinois
Address: 1058 West Washington Boulevard, Chicago, IL
60607-2103
Phone: (312) 591-9222
Website: www.oprah.com

Ghost Lore

Oprah Winfrey—she is one of the richest and most famous women
in the world. She is the Emmy Award-winning host of *The Oprah
Winfrey Show,* the highest-rated talk show in television history. She
is an Academy Award-nominated actress. She is a successful entre-
preneur, magazine publisher, and the world's only black billionaire.

What most people don't know about Oprah is that her famous
Harpo Studios is said to be haunted by the ghost of the "Gray Lady"
and other spirits.

- Mysterious sounds: footsteps, laughing children, crying children, whispering voices, loud crashing, clinking of glasses, and music.

- The scent of violets or a violet-scented perfume.

- Doors open and close on their own.

- Lights turn on and off.

- Files and other objects are moved around overnight.

- An apparition of a woman decked out in a gray dress and old-fashioned hat.

History

1892 – Chicago's Second Regiment Armory was built at Aberdeen and Washington.

1915 – The Eastland Disaster. Hundreds of men, women, and children died when the S.S. Eastland overturned in the Chicago River.

More than 200 of the bodies were taken to a cold-storage warehouse in the Second Regiment Armory which was being used as a temporary morgue for the victims.

1943 – The armory was converted into a skating rink called the Roller Bowl. It was also used for parties and special events.

1958 – The skating rink was remodeled and used as the Fred Niles Studios where they filmed movies such as *Mickey One* (1965) starring Warren Beatty, television programs such as *The Monkees* (1966-68) and *Mutual of Omaha's Wild Kingdom (1963-1988)*, and commercials with Muhammad Ali.

1984 – It became Studio Network Inc.

1984 – Oprah Winfrey moved to Chicago to host the WLS-TV program *AM Chicago* which later became *The Oprah Winfrey Show.*

1988 – Winfrey purchased the building and established Harpo Studios, making her the third woman in the American entertainment industry (after Mary Pickford and Lucille Ball) to own her own studio.

Investigation

Many of the employees at Harpo Studios are convinced that the building is haunted by the victims of the Eastland Disaster. Since the first day they opened the studio, the workers have experienced strange sounds and haunting activity. Many of them refuse to be in the building at night.

Most often, they report sightings of the "Gray Lady," a shadowy apparition of a woman dressed in an old-fashioned, flowing gray dress and wearing a large ornate hat. She appears to float down the corridors after dark. The overnight guards even claim to have seen her on their security monitors.

Others have told us about hearing the sounds of ghostly children who laugh, cry, and walk the hallways. Many of the victims of the 1915 Eastland Disaster were young. Their tiny corpses were laid out in the temporary morgue until they could be identified by family members.

We were told that Oprah openly discussed the haunting on one of the early episodes of her program but has since refused to talk about it. It is speculated that she fears it would scare away her studio audiences and guests if they knew about the ghosts.

Saint Valentine's Day Massacre

Location: Chicago, Cook County, Illinois
Address: 2122 North Clark Street, Chicago, IL 60614

Ghost Lore

Saint Valentine's Day, the day traditionally associated with romantic love, was sullied by violence during one of Chicago's most famous gangland murders. Al Capone, the gangster, was responsible for the slaying of seven men from a rival gang. Negative energy from that day still permeates the site of this massacre, and troubled spirits still wander the grounds.

- Feelings of trepidation.

- The sounds of machine guns.

- Mysterious screams, sobs, and moaning sounds.

- Dogs growl and cower in fear. Animals generally avoid the area.

History

1893 – George Clarence Moran, later to be known as "Bugs," was born in Minnesota, just outside the Twin Cities.

1899 – Alphonse Gabriel Capone, later to be known as "Scarface," was born in Brooklyn, NY.

1919 – Capone moved to Chicago.

1920 – National Prohibition began when the Eighteenth Amendment went into effect. This resulted in bootlegging and organized crime. Capone established his crime syndicate known as the Chicago Outfit and developed a monopoly on the organized crime in Chicago.

1923 – Moran moved to Chicago and along with Dion

"Deanie""O'Banion, Vincent "The Schemer" Drucci, and Earl "Hymie" Weiss established the North Side Gang.

1929 – February 14. Saint Valentine's Day Massacre.

1930 – Capone became "Public Enemy Number One" on the Chicago Crime Commission's list. Moran was number six on the list.

1931 – Capone was convicted of income tax evasion and sentenced to prison for eleven years.

1947 – Capone died of complications related to syphilis.

1949 – The SMG garage was used as an antique furniture business.

1957 – Moran was convicted of bank robbery and sentenced to ten years in prison. He died 45 days after entering Leavenworth Penitentiary.

1967 – The SMG garage was demolished, but the wall where the massacre happened was preserved and put up for auction. Canadian businessman George Patey (1927-2004) was the highest bidder. He moved the 412 bricks from the six-feet-high by ten-feet-wide wall to Canada and put them on exhibit.

1972 – Paley opened the Banjo Palace, a nightclub in Vancouver, and put the wall on display in the men's room.

1976 – The Banjo Palace closed.

1997 – Paley sold the wall, brick by brick.

Investigation

The Irish/German North Side Gang headed by Bugs Moran controlled northern Chicago while the south side was controlled by Al Capone's Italian gang—the Outfit. When Moran began muscling in on the southern territory, Capone decided to put a stop to it and quickly hatched a plot. Capone had a gangster friend in Detroit arrange a deal with Moran to sell him some illegal Canadian liquor. The delivery was to be made in the SMG Cartage Company garage at 2122 North Street on February 14 at 10:30 am. While Moran's men waited inside the garage, Capone's men pulled up in a stolen patty wagon. Three of Capone's men were dressed in stolen police uniforms, and two were dressed in street clothes. Moran's ill-fated men, thinking it was a routine police bust, compliantly dropped their weapons and put their hands on the wall, when ordered to do so. Whereupon Capone's men pulled out Thompson submachine guns and opened fire, killing all seven men. Moran, who was the main target of this assault, arrived late and hightailed it when he saw the paddy wagon parked outside. Capone had an alibi and avoided arrest, since he was conveniently vacationing in Florida at the time of the massacre.

One of the murdered gangsters, John May, was Moran's mechanic. At the time of the massacre, he was working on a truck and had his beloved Alsatian dog, named Highball, tied to the axle. After the shooting, neighbors could hear the dog barking frantically. When they checked on the dog, they discovered the grisly crime scene. The dog was the only surviving witness and was so disturbed that it later had to be put down.

Another gangster killed at the massacre was Moran's brother-in-law, James Clark. Ever since that fateful day, Capone believed Clark's vengeful ghost was stalking and haunting him.

Today the garage is gone, and what remains is a fenced-off lawn that belongs to the nearby nursing home. Many people believe the dead gangsters still remain to haunt the area. People hear ghostly sounds of machine guns and agonizing screams. A group of seven shadowy apparitions have been seen. Dogs are reportedly spooked by the location; perhaps they sense the trauma experienced by Highball.

After the SMG garage was demolished, the wall where the gang-sters were lined up and executed was preserved and auctioned off. George Patey, a Canadian businessman, was the highest bidder and brought the wall, with its bloodstains and bullet holes, to Vancouver, Canada, and put it on exhibit. Later, he opened the Banjo Palace nightclub and assembled the wall in the men's room. After the nightclub closed, he sold individual bricks online for $2500-3000 each. It is said the bricks were haunted with the neg-ative energy of the massacre, since many of the people who bought them were later cursed with death, disease, divorce, bankruptcy, and other misfortune.

Mount Carmel Cemetery

Location: Hillside, Cook County, Illinois
Official Name: Mount Carmel Catholic Cemetery
Affiliation: Catholic
Address: 1400 South Wolf Road, Hillside, IL 60162-2105
Phone: (708) 449-8300

The Italian Bride: From the Harrison Ave. entrance, take your first left. Pass by the administration building on your left, and the bride will be on your right. (Section A)
Al Capone: From the Roosevelt entrance, take your first right (Section 35) and Capone will be on your right side.

Ghost Lore

It is said that both saints and sinners are buried in Mount Carmel Cemetery and that together they haunt the cemetery at night.

- Apparitions of the Italian Bride wearing a glowing, white wedding dress are seen wandering the cemetery.

- At night, her grave will glow brightly.

- A mysterious scent of fresh roses, even in the winter.

- Apparitions of Al Capone are seen near his grave.

History

1901 – The cemetery was consecrated.

1921 – Julia Buccola Petta died in Schaumburg of apparent complications from childbirth and was buried in Mount Carmel Cemetery with her stillborn infant.

1927 – Julia's mother, Philomena Buccola, had visions of Julia pleading to be dug up. She persuaded the authorities to exhume the body.

1947 – Mobster Al Capone died and was buried in Mount Carmel Cemetery.

Investigation

The Italian Bride. A young Sicilian woman, Julia Buccola Petta, died during childbirth in 1921. It was a Sicilian custom for women who died during childbirth to be buried in their wedding dresses. The family dressed her in her white gown and buried both her and her stillborn infant in the same grave at Mount Carmel Cemetery.

Soon after her death, her mother began having recurring dreams of Julia. In the visions, the daughter appeared to the mother, claiming to still be alive and pleading to be dug up. After six years of petitioning the church, the officials finally consented to the mother's wishes and allowed the grave to be exhumed.

When the rotting casket was hauled up and opened, onlookers were shocked to find the corpse perfectly preserved. After six years of being in the ground, the body had not decomposed. No explanation was ever found for this apparent miracle. Before the body was reinterred, one of the astonished witnesses photographed the corpse bride. In the picture, which was later displayed on the grave, Julia appears to be alive and merely sleeping. The Italian inscription reads, "Questa fotografia presa dopo 6 anni morta," which roughly translates as, "This photograph was taken six years after this woman's death." Later, a life-sized statue of the bride in her wedding dress holding a bouquet of roses was erected in her honor at the grave.

In the years since the disinterment, numerous witnesses have seen the phantom bride in her white dress either standing near the grave or wandering among the gravestones. In his book, *Windy City Ghosts,* Dale Kaczmarek recounts a sighting when witnesses saw the bride walking through the cemetery during a rainstorm. On closer inspection, they noticed her hair and dress were completely dry, despite the fact she was in the pouring rain.

In her book, *Chicago Haunts,* Ursula Bielski tells a story of a young boy who was accidentally left behind in the cemetery. When his family realized he was missing, they rushed back to the cemetery to look for him. Eventually, they spotted him near a grave, holding the hand of a woman in white. As they ran to retrieve the boy, they were startled to see the mysterious woman vanish before their eyes.

Many visitors to the grave have reported the scent of fresh-cut roses. This unexplained aroma has even been noted in the dead of winter, when it was obvious no fresh flowers were present.

Al Capone. While living at his home in Miami, Florida, "Public Enemy Number One," Al Capone, died in 1947 from complications related to syphilis. He was originally buried in Mount Olivet Cemetery in Chicago, but, due to problems with vandalism, his casket was later dug up and secretly reinterred at Mount Carmel Cemetery. The original tombstone was left at Mount Olivet Cemetery as a decoy, but people soon discovered the new burial spot. Instead of desecrating this grave, people from around the world would visit and leave tokens such as coins, beer bottles, cigars, and flowers. Some of the visitors have reported the feeling of not being alone and of being watched. A few have had ghostly encounters with the deceased gangster and have even seen his apparition standing near the grave.

Resurrection Mary

Location: Justice, Cook County, Illinois
Official Name: Resurrection Cemetery & Mausoleums
Address: 7200 Archer Road, Justice, IL 60458-1139
Phone: (708) 458-4770

Ghost Lore

Stories of vanishing hitchhikers have been told for hundreds of years, but none as famous as the story of Resurrection Mary. This legend has inspired songs, a novel, and even a motion picture. The story is told that in the 1930s a beautiful young woman with blonde hair and blue eyes died on Archer Road. She was on her way home after a night of dancing at a local ballroom when she was killed either in a car accident or as the victim of a hit-and-run. To this day, the ghost of Mary haunts both Archer Road and Resurrection Cemetery where she's buried.

- After an evening of dancing, men will drive Mary home only to have her vanish from the car as they drive past Resurrection Cemetery.

- Men will pick up a hitchhiking woman and give her a ride home. To their amazement, she will vanish from the car as they drive past Resurrection Cemetery.

- Motorists driving past Resurrection Cemetery will accidentally strike a young woman who darts out in front of their cars, but a body is never found.

- Mary can sometimes be seen wandering inside the cemetery at night.

History

1904 – Resurrection Cemetery was consecrated.

1927 – Anna Mary Norkus was killed and buried in Resurrection Cemetery.

1930 – Mary Miskowski was killed by a hit-and-run driver and buried in Resurrection Cemetery.

1934 – Mary Bregovy, 21, was killed in a car accident and buried in Resurrection Cemetery. The first known sightings of the ghost known as Resurrection Mary occurred that same year.

1939 – Jerry Palus encountered Resurrection Mary.

1973 – Resurrection Mary was encountered at Harlow's Nightclub and Chet's Melody Lounge.

1976 – The bars to the Resurrection Cemetery gate were found pulled apart and bent.

1994 – The story of Resurrection Mary was featured on *Unsolved Mysteries*.

Investigation

The Sightings. In 1939, a man named Jerry Palus (1914-1992) was at the Liberty Grove Hall and Ballroom in Brighton Park. He considered himself to be something of a lady's man, and asked an attractive, blue-eyed, blonde-haired girl to dance. They danced together for most of the evening. She told Palus her name was Mary. Palus later recalled that she wasn't very talkative and her hands were cold as ice. He offered to drive her home after the dance, and she said she lived on Damen Avenue, but directed him to drive down Archer Road. As they passed Resurrection Cemetery, she asked him to stop the car. Whereupon, she got out of the vehicle, walked towards the cemetery gates, and vanished before his eyes. The next day, he drove to the address on Damen Avenue, and Mary's mother answered the door and explained to him that Mary had died five years earlier. She showed him a picture of Mary, and he recognized her as being the same girl with whom he had danced the night before. He had previously worked in a funeral home, and it was at this point that he realized why her hands had been ice cold. to the touch—it was the touch of a corpse!

In January of 1979, a taxi driver driving down Archer Road was lost. He noticed a blonde-haired woman in a white dress walking on the side of the road and offered to give her a free ride if she could give him directions back to town. She got in the cab, and he drove about a mile down the road when she asked him to stop in front of Resurrection Cemetery. When he glanced over toward his passenger, he noticed she had vanished from his cab, but the door had never opened. He was just one of many cabbies to give a ride to the phantom fare.

In September of 1980, a woman by the name of Clare Lopez-Rudnicki, her husband Mark A. Rudnicki, and two friends were driving down Archer Road when they saw a glowing, white figure slowly walking on the shoulder of the road. As they passed her, they looked back and noticed she had no face—just a black hole.

In October of 1989, Janet L. Kalal and Pamela Turlow-Wilson were driving past Resurrection Cemetery, when a woman in white darted out in front of their vehicle. They believed they had hit her, but there was no impact, no sound, and no body.

Description. She is described as a young woman between the ages of eighteen and twenty-one, with blonde hair and blue eyes. Wearing a long, white ball gown and dancing shoes. In some accounts, she wears a thin shawl.

The Gate. On the night of August 10, 1976, a motorist driving past Resurrection Cemetery spotted the "glowing figure" of a woman pulling at the bars of the cemetery gate as if she were locked inside and trying to get out. He immediately reported it to the Justice Police Department. When police officer Pat Homa responded to the call, he didn't find the girl in the cemetery. However, what he did find was that the bars on the gate, where she had been seen, were scorched and had been bent as if somebody with supernatural strength had pried them apart. He also found what appeared to be small handprints with skin-like texture embedded into the twisted metal.

The cemetery board offered the implausible explanation that the bars were inadvertently bent by workers who carelessly backed a truck into the gate. The bars were removed, straightened, and returned in 1978, but the discoloration and imprint of fingers still remained. Eventually the board replaced the entire gate, and nobody knows what became of the original bars. To this day, nobody has been able to offer a rational explanation for the marks on the bars.

Who was Mary?

There are several theories as to the identity of this woman. Over the years, several candidates have been suggested by researchers:

* Mary Bregovy, a 21-year-old Polish girl who liked to frequent the dance halls. She was killed in an auto accident in downtown Chicago on March 10, 1934 and buried in her favorite gown in Resurrection Cemetery. Her address was 4611 South Damen Avenue, which is consistent with Jerry Palus' account.

  Problems: This Mary had short, dark hair and was buried in an orchid-colored dress; however, witnesses describe Resurrection Mary as having blonde hair and wearing a white dress. Moreover, this Mary died on Wacker Drive, not Archer Avenue, and it's not likely she was on her way to or from a dance hall.

* Mary, a young Polish girl who was killed in the 1940s when she crashed her parents' car near Resurrection Cemetery in the early morning hours while on her way to meet her boyfriend in Willow Springs. Supposedly, she was buried in a term grave in Resurrection Cemetery.

  Problem: This Mary died in the 1940s; however, the first sightings of Resurrection Mary occurred earlier, in the 1930s.

* Mary Miskowski from Bridgeport. She was killed while crossing Archer Avenue to attend a Halloween costume party in the 1930s.

* Mary Duranski, a woman killed in a 1934 car accident while on her way home from a dance.

- Mary, a girl who was killed in 1936 on Archer Avenue while on her way home from the Oh Henry Ballroom. The black Model A sedan she was riding in collided with a farm truck.

- Marija, a 12-year-old Lithuanian girl named Anna Norkus who was killed in 1927. She was tall for her age, blonde, liked to dance, and was known by her middle name, Marija (Mary). For her birthday, her father took her to the Oh Henry Ballroom. On the way home, they were in a fatal auto accident near Resurrection Cemetery.

  Problems: First, Marija was actually buried in Saint Casimir Cemetery, although some claim she may have been temporarily interred in Resurrection Cemetery. Second, according to eyewitness accounts, Resurrection Mary was not a twelve-year-old girl. She appeared to be somewhere between eighteen and twenty-one years of age.

Notes. In Section MM, Site 9819, at Resurrection Cemetery, there is a gravestone for Mary Bregovy (1888-1922), a 34-year-old mother. This is not the same Mary Bregovy as the single woman who died in 1934 at the age of 21.

After years of curiosity seekers, the cemetery has adopted the official position of not commenting on the legend of Resurrection Mary. The employees we spoke with upheld this policy, even though they helped direct us to several graves thought to be "Mary."

The Dare. If you drive down Archer Road, you might encounter Resurrection Mary. She is usually seen during the months of October, November, and December. Often the sightings occur when it is either raining or snowing. The most frequent time people see her is around 1:30 am.

Bachelor's Grove Cemetery

Location: Midlothian, Cook County, Illinois
Address: 143rd Street and Midlothian Turnpike, Midlothian, IL 60445

Directions: From Midlothian, take US-45S to 143rd St. Turn left on 143rd St. and follow it until you see the Rubio Woods (Cook County Forest Preserve) sign and parking area. Park your car there and walk across the street towards the large phone towers. The trail to the cemetery is just to the right of the towers. Follow the trail back a bit and the cemetery will be on your right-hand side.

Ghost Lore

Many believe this is the most haunted cemetery in the nation, and some would even say in the entire world. Bachelor's Grove Cemetery has been extensively written about and featured on several television programs. It's long history of satanic rituals, vandal-

115

ism, and desecration of graves has without doubt disturbed the dead. Consequently, hundreds have people have visited this grave-yard and reported a wide variety of truly bizarre haunting experiences:

- Mysterious colored lights.

- Strange ghostly sounds. People have heard the name "Minna" being called out. Indeed, there is a gravestone with that name on it.

- A vanishing haunted house.

- Trees that violently shake when no wind is blowing.

- Phantom cars that appear and disappear.

- Faces in the mist.

- Cold spots.

- Apparitions of the "White Lady," a farmer, a glowing man wearing a yellow suit and hat, and a two-headed monster.

History

1820s – Bachelor's Grove was settled.

1844 – Bachelor's Grove Cemetery was established with Eliza (Mr.s Leonard H.) Scott being the first burial.

1935 – William B. Nobles was the last full burial.

Early 1960s – The entrance road, formerly a branch of the Midlothian Turnpike, was closed off, causing the cemetery to become isolated. This attracted vandalism and satanic rituals. Originally the cemetery had about 200 tombstones, but almost 90% of them were stolen or damaged. It's believed some of the tombstones were tossed into a nearby pond.

1973 – Seven teenagers were arrested when police caught them digging up a grave.

1976 – Clarence Fulton, 74, a descendant of one of the original set-

tlers of Bachelor's Grove, was the last surviving trustee of the cemetery. He handed over control of the cemetery to the Cook County Board.

1989 – Robert E. Shields was cremated and his ashes were buried in the family plot. This was the last known disposition of human remains at Bachelor's Grove Cemetery.

1991 – Paranormal investigator Jude Huff-Felz snapped the famous "Madonna of Bachelor's Grove" photo.

Investigation

The cemetery has had a long history of desecration. In the 1930s, gangsters disposed of murder victims and illegal firearms in the nearby pond. In the 1960s, satanic cults performed rituals there. In the 1970s and beyond, troublemakers littered and vandalized the cemetery. Some have even attempted to rob the graves. There are plenty of reasons for the spirits here to be restless and disturbed, and people have told us a variety of strange stories.

The Madonna of Bachelor's Grove. Many witnesses claim to see the apparition known as the "White Lady," also known as "Mrs. Rogers." She is usually carrying a baby or looking for a lost child. On August 10, 1991, the Ghost Research Society was conducting an investigation at Bachelor's Grove Cemetery when researcher Jude Huff-Felz photographed the famous White Lady seated on a checkered plinth. The investigative team was getting unusual readings on some of their equipment in that particular region of the cemetery. This prompted Huff-Felz to snap an infrared picture in that direction. The image clearly showed a semi-transparent, seated woman wearing old-fashioned clothing. The photo has appeared in numerous publications, including the *National Examiner* and *Chicago Sun-Times,* and been featured on several television programs.

Phantom Cars. Although the main road has been rerouted, people frequently see ghost cars that appear out of nowhere, then disappear just as quickly. Often, witnesses have to jump out of the way to avoid being hit by the cars. Sometimes they're not fast enough, but the phantom car just passes through their body without any impact.

Bizarre Ghosts. Besides the White Lady, people also report seeing a monstrous two-headed man. Often he's swimming in the pond. Also near the pond, witnesses have seen a phantom farmer with a horse and plow. The story is that in the 1870s a farmer's horse was spooked and pulled him into the water where both drowned.

Spook Lights. Baseball-sized orbs of light are often seen floating through the graveyard. The lights, usually colored red or blue, will dart past startled onlookers, then playfully dance around the gravestones.

The Vanishing House. Occasionally, people visiting the grounds at night will see a mysterious house in the woods behind the cemetery. It's usually described as a white Victorian farmhouse with a porch swing and surrounded by a picket fence. They claim see a light shining through the front window. Those who are brave enough will try to get closer to get a better look, but the house disappears before they can reach it. It is said that one teenager did succeed in reaching the house and entering it, but he never came back out. When his friends returned the next day, the house could not be found. Checking at the courthouse, we were unable to find any records indicating that there had ever been a house in that location.

The Dare. If you see the vanishing house and manage to enter it, you will never return.

Willowbrook Ballroom

Location: Willow Springs, Cook County, Illinois
Correction: The former name was Oh Henry; not O'Henry or O. Henry as some sources claim.
Address: 8900 Archer Avenue, Willow Springs, IL 60480-1206
Phone: (708) 839-1000
Fax: (708) 839-1005
E-mail: willowbrookballroom@comcast.net
Website: www.willowbrookballroom.com

Ghost Lore

Although her true identity is a subject of debate, most paranormal investigators agree that whoever she was, Resurrection Mary loved to dance. It is believed that one of the places she frequented was the Oh Henry Ballroom, known today as the Willowbrook Ballroom. It's rumored that in the years since her untimely death, young Mary will still occasionally visit her favorite ballroom and wait for some unsuspecting young men to ask her to dance.

History

1920 – John Verderbar sought to turn his five acres of pristine rural land into a prized weekend retreat for tourists. John's 19-year-old son Rudy convinced him that the family's five-acre land would be better served as a dance hall.

1921 – The Oh Henry Park was constructed by John and Rudy Verderbar. The park featured a large picnic area and included a 40-by-65 foot dance floor. Interestingly, the startup cost of the park was partially sponsored by the Williamson Candy Company, the maker of the Oh Henry candy bar.

1923 – The Oh Henry open pavilion was expanded and became completely enclosed.

1930 – The Oh Henry was completely consumed by a roaring fire that burned the dance hall to the ground.

1930 – Almost immediately, the Oh Henry park was rebuilt by a massive force of over 200 carpenters. The cost of the the new park nearly climbed to a staggering $100,000.

1931 – The Oh Henry Ballroom was crammed with over 1,700 invited guests who showed up to celebrate the grand re-opening.

1940 – The dance hall proudly announced that the state-of-the-art hall was now equipped with air conditioning. It was during this time that the owner's advertising agreement with the Oh Henry candy bar had run out, and the owners decided to rename the place "The Willows." However, the public's response was overwhelmingly negative. Finally, the owners sided with their customers and the name remained Oh Henry.

1955 – In order to keep up with the changing tastes of the time, the Verderbar's added a 20,000-square-foot restaurant called the Willowbrook Room. In addition to the restaurant, a large Carousel Bar was also added.

1959 – The Oh Henry was officially changed to reflect the growth and prestige of the business. The building was re-named the Willowbrook.

1967 – John Verderbar died at the age of 91.

1997 – The Verderbar family sold the establishment to the Jodwalis family.

Currently – The Willowbrook continues to house dances and weddings

Investigation

While giving us a tour of the ballroom, the owner of the Willowbrook Ballroom informed us that she often has people stopping in to inquire about the legend. She tells them that according to the story, it was indeed the Oh Henry Ballroom that Mary left the night she died.

Since the 1930s, the ghost wearing a white dress and dancing shoes continues to be seen at this ballroom. She will dance with young men and ask them to drive her home, but when they pass by Resurrection Cemetery, she disappears from their car.

NORTHERN ILLINOIS

Death Curve

Location: Cambridge, Henry County, Illinois

Directions: The cemetery and Devil Curve are near each other.

To Devil Curve: From Cambridge take S West St. towards the middle school. Turn right on South Rd. Turn left on 1200E. Turn right on Timber Ridge (950 N) and in a little over 1 mile you will come to a sharp left turn in the road. This is Devil Curve, and there will be a fence post and big tree to your right. The old farmhouse and barn were located on the land behind the fence post and tree.

To Rosedale Cemetery: From Cambridge, take S West St. towards the middle school. Turn right on South Rd. Turn left on 1200E. The cemetery will be on your right. Take the last cemetery entrance and about half way in you will see a large Cannon Gravestone. From there walk towards the telephone pole on your left near the cornfield. The unmarked graves are just to the left of the field. You will see an indentation in the ground near the graves of William Currier and Rose Margaret Sanders.

Ghost Lore

In the early 1900s a woman lived with her husband and their seven children in a farmhouse just outside the town of Cambridge. The husband came down with a terrible cold that eventually led to his death. Overcome with grief and despair, the woman felt helpless and inept at raising the children on her own. Drowning in misery, the woman snapped and decided that the only way to rectify the situation, was to kill her children. Following through with her plan,

she one by one decapitated all seven of her children with an axe. Once the crime was committed, the woman immediately realized she was responsible for the horrific act. Unable to live with herself, the woman set the house on fire. Once the house was on fire, the woman grabbed the shotgun, placed it to her head, and pulled the trigger, killing herself at 10:27 p.m. The bodies of the woman and her children are buried in a nearby cemetery.

- Those who go to the "Devil Curve" at 10:27 p.m. will see the ghost of the murderous woman sitting on the fence post in front of where her house once stood.

- Many automobile accidents at Devil Curve have been caused by the angry spirit of the woman.

- What was left of the charred bodies of the children were all stuffed into one unmarked grave in a nearby cemetery.

History

1873 – Julia Johnson was born in Andover, Illinois.

1896 – Julia married a Mr. Clarence Markham.

1905 – Julia Markham killed herself and family.

1914 – It is believed that Mr. Markham remarried.

1951 – Clarence Markham passed away at the age of 77.

1990s – The old Markham barn burned down either by accident or on purpose.

Investigation

The ghost lore is somewhat close to the truth on this case, but here is how the tragic story really happened:

In October 1905, Mrs. Julia Markham took the lives of her seven children. One morning at approximately 11 a.m., Julia sent her two oldest and strongest children off to fetch some water so they would

be out of the way for what she was about to do. While the two oldest children were gone she grabbed the family axe, and methodically went to each of her five children and struck them in the head with the axe. A few moments later when the two oldest children retuned with the water, she continued her frenzied rampage by taking the axe to them as well.

Once all of the children had met their fate by the hands of the axe, Mrs. Markham calmly grabbed a butcher knife from the kitchen and tried to end her own life. However, she was not so lucky, as the knife she grabbed was a bit dull and the wound did not kill her. She then rounded up the lifeless bodies of her children and placed them down on the bed and doused them, and the room, with coal oil and set the house ablaze. Immediately the wooden house was engulfed in flames and Mrs. Markham hoped that she would die in the fire. Yet only after being in the burning house for a few minutes, the heat became too much for her to take, and she stumbled out the home severally burned. By this time, neighbors had spotted the fire and came to the rescue. When they arrived, they were horrified at what they saw. A doctor was called to the fire to look

after Mrs. Markham, who first denied that she had been responsible for the deaths or the fire. By the time the doctor got there, she had confessed to the grizzly murders. At 3 p.m. Mrs. Markham died from her various wounds.

The father and husband, Clarence Markham, did not die of some illness. During the murders he was working at a nearby farm, and when he returned home for the day he was terrified by what he found. According to the *Cambridge Chronicle,* Mrs. Markham had a history of suicidal behavior, as ten years prior she tried to take her own life by throwing herself into a well. Her attempt at suicide failed when she was "saved" by rescuers who believed she had accidentally fallen into the well. Those who knew her before she was married shared the firm belief that she was not a mentally strong person.

Later that day a mail carrier on his route found a letter in a nearby mailbox addressed to Mr. Markham. According to the *Cambridge Chronicle,* the letter provided proof that the murders were premeditated and not an act of rage or a temporary bout of insanity. The letter read:

"Dear Clarence: This is to say goodbye to you. Some give their souls for others, and I will do this for my children. God bless them! They will all die happy in the arms of Jesus. I will meet them there, and some day you will join us too."

Due to finances, all the seven children could not be buried separately, so Mrs. Markham was buried in one grave, while what was left of her seven burned children was all dumped into another grave. Both unmarked graves can still be found in Rosedale Cemetery.

Unfortunately, the Markham farmhouse where the murders took place burned down many years ago. In front of where the house once stood is the infamous "Devil Curve," where the ghost of Mrs. Markham is said to haunt. The normally straight road makes a sharp left turn which is said to be the location for many unexplained accidents.

The story of Mrs. Markham and the haunting has been circulating

the region for many years. We spoke with numerous residents that recalled that when they were kids they were told stories warning them about the cursed Devil Curve.

Much of the ghostly activity seems to surround the fence post near the side of Devil Curve.

One woman who visited the site with her friends when she was in high school told us her eerie story. The year was 1988, and the young woman finally garnered up enough courage to visit Devil Curve, the place that all of her friends were talking about. While several of the friends went walking through the land, looking for the ghost of Mrs. Markham, the woman decided to hang back in the car, afraid that something may happen. While she was nervously watching the field, she was amazed to see something white float off the fence post and move into the cornfield and disappear into the darkness.

Another woman told us that while she was visiting Devil Curve, she noticed a strange small light dancing around the area. Terrified at what she was looking at, she did not stick around long enough to find out what it was.

The Dare. If you are brave enough to travel to Devil Curve at night, you will encounter the ghosts of the murdered children or even the spirit of Mrs. Markham herself.

Galena Historical Museum

Location: Galena, Jo Daviess County, Illinois
Address: 211 South Bench Street, Galena, IL 61036-2203
Phone: (815) 777-9129
Fax: (815) 777-9131
E-mail: info@galenahistorymuseum.org
Website: www.galenahistorymuseum.org

Directions: From South Main St., turn left on Hill St. Turn left on South Bench St. and arrive at the museum.

Ghost Lore

One of the main goals for many historical museums is to ensure that they keep the past alive for future generations to enjoy and learn from. By doing this, visitors are afforded the opportunity to get a glimpse of how life was lived in a time period outside of the one in which they are living. However, the Galena Historic

Museum may be doing too good of a job of keeping the past alive, because not only do they have over 10,000 items from the past, they actually have a spirit or two as well.

- The historic building is haunted by several ghosts that like to make themselves known to both visitors and workers.

- Phantom footsteps are often heard, but never seen, in the museum.

- So much paranormal activity happens in the museum that staff had to start a journal in order to keep track of all the mysterious happenings.

History

1856 – The home of Daniel Barrows was burned in the Great Galena Fire.

1858 – Barrows hired an architect by the name of William Dennison to design his home.

1859 – Construction of Barrows new home was completed.

1883 – Mr. Barrows suffered some financially hard times and eventually defaulted on his home.

1883 – S. O. Stillman received the home from Barrows.

1885 – The home was purchased by John Ross.

1922 – The home once again changed hands when it was sold to the Widely Lodge of the IOOF (International Order of Odd Fellows).

1922 – The IOOF started renovating the home, which was in need of many repairs and modifications.

1938 – Partly due to the high cost of renovating the home, the IOOF decided to free itself of the burden and sold the home to the City of Galena.

1938 – The Galena Museum Association was formed and signed a 99-year lease on the home.

1938 – The Galena City Hall moved into the front of the building.

1967 – The City Hall moved out of the building.

Currently – The Galena Museum occupies the building.

Investigation

The former Museum Director, Daryl Watson, wrote in his book Ghosts of Galena that in 1989, the museum staff began to sense that there was something strange happening in their building. Looking for some explanation for the odd events occurring in the building, the staff discovered a story about a strange event that took place back when the City Hall still occupied part of the building. It was here during a meeting that several residents heard a loud commotion coming from the upstairs hallway. Knowing that no one else was thought to be in the building, they rushed upstairs and found the hallway completely empty. A group searched the rest of the building to no avail, as and no one was found.

After witnessing many unexplainable events the museum staff started compiling a journal of paranormal activity that was happening inside the building. Watson writes of a party that was held in the building where the service staff working that evening experienced some ghostly activity. During the party champagne was being served to the guests, yet many of the servers reported that the plastic glasses sitting on their trays would simply fall to the floor for no apparent reason. The manager chalked this up to the simple clumsiness of the staff. However, after several lost trays of champagne, the manager started to think that maybe the workers were not so clumsy and that something strange may be happening. The director was not alone in his new belief, as several other guests watched a few glasses that were sitting on the table inexplicably fall to the floor, as though guided by some unseen hands.

Upon our visit to the museum we spoke with an employee that recalled several strange events that took place in the building. The woman stated that although she did not have any personal experiences in the building, plenty of other employees had. She stated that nearly all of the staff working there reported hearing weird noises throughout the building. These mysterious noises seem to occur so often that many staff now just simply shrug it off as though it is normal everyday occurrence.

The most commonly reported paranormal experience at the museum seems to happen to employees while they are working alone at the museum. While busy at work, employees often hear the sound of someone walking up and down the stairs. Thinking that someone else must have come in unnoticed, the employees go to the staircase only to find that no one is there, and the mysterious footsteps have simply stopped.

Another odd aspect of the building involves the alarm system. Many times throughout the years the alarm system has gone off during the night. Those responding to the alarm often accept that the alarm was triggered by burglars, birds, rats, or other animals in the building. Yet every time a search of the building is conducted, no cause for the "alarm" can be found and the staff are left baffled.

Other employees report that while working alone at night, they often hear the second floor furniture being moved around. Curious as to what may be causing the noise, they race up the stairs to find that not only has the furniture not been moved, but the sound has mysteriously ceased.

Old Salem Cemetery

Location: Lacon, Marshall County, Illinois

Directions: Take Washburn Rd. out of town. It turns into 1475 E. At the stop sign go straight. The road will be Wind Haven Rd. Turn right on Sun Rd. When you see the Hill sign, take the dirt road to the right, and the cemetery will be straight ahead.

Ghost Lore

One of the most secluded cemeteries in this book is the Old Salem Cemetery, which is hidden way out in the middle of the country where the spirits can roam free. Just by finding this place, you should get a pat on the back or at least a job with Map Quest. However, finding this out of the way place is the easy part; the hard part seems to be leaving. Many visitors report strange mechanical problems with their vehicles when they try to leave. From dead batteries, stalled engines, and mysterious starter failures, it seems that the spirits of this cemetery do not want you to leave.

Locals tell of a young girl who suffered a painful death when she burned to death in a tragic house fire. What was left of her body was buried in the cemetery. When you go to her grave with a book of matches, she will make herself known to you.

The cemetery has the distinction of being the oldest cemetery in the region.

History

1834 – According to the book *Marshall County Illinois Township History*, the cemetery was started when 18-year-old Mary Conley was buried in a plot on the land. The cemetery land had been given to the town by Nathan Owen.

1850 – Locals reported that the cemetery was in rough shape and was overrun with weed grasses and brush.

1890 – A fence was constructed around the cemetery to help control the maintenance of the place.

1917 – The cemetery association was formed. The goal of the association was to raise funds for upkeep and maintenance of the cemetery. Until this time, individual families were responsible for taking care of their own plots.

1920 – The cemetery association met at in the Belsly Implement Store to elect officers.

1928 – The original run down fence was replaced with a stronger sturdy fence.

1930 – A third fence was constructed to close off the land deeded to the cemetery by Mark Belsly.

1951 – The cemetery association was revamped and a caretaker was hired to maintain the grounds.

1966 – The cemetery land was surveyed, a new area was plotted, and grave plots were sold to future residents.

Investigation

The Old Salem Cemetery is not the oldest cemetery in the region—it is actually the third oldest cemetery in Marshall County. According to the caretaker, 323 known people are buried in the cemetery, with at least a handful of unknown bodies. Many of the graves in the cemetery date back over a hundred years, although new burials are still being accepted.

For you romantics, there is a man buried in the cemetery that was the only person in Marshall County to list the date of his marriage on the tombstone.

The stories of the cemetery being haunted are not new; we have tracked mysterious tales of the cemetery back at least 50 years.

We spoke with the caretaker of the cemetery, who told us that during the 1850-1860s the railroad was constructing a track through the area. Unfortunately, many of the workers died in accidents that commonly took place during construction. Many of these accidents were caused by a lack of safe working conditions. The railroad was looking to bury the bodies as cheaply and quickly as they could. It was decided that the bodies of the fallen workers would be dumped into a mass unmarked grave. The evidence of this mass burial can still be seen today. If you get to the cemetery as the sun comes up in the morning, you will be able to see the indentation of their graves running along the left side fence that encloses the cemetery.

The caretaker also informed us that on cool fall days, the cemetery gets foggy and steam rises from the ground.

Another phenomenon of the cemetery is the mysterious complications that visitors often notice when they try to leave the area. The lore states that these problems are caused by the spirits of the cemetery refusing to let visitors leave the cemetery. Oftentimes vehicles that normally run fine, start to act up and refuse to start. Visitors

seemed plagued by dead batteries, electrical problems, and vehicles that simply shut down and refuse to start back up. In the 1990s the town was said to have had trouble with a Devil worshipping cult that used the cemetery for their sinister rituals.

The Dare. One of the more fascinating stories of the cemetery states that buried somewhere in the cemetery there is a girl that was burned to death in a fire. If you visit her grave and try to light a match, the match will not light, no matter how many times you try to light it.

Kaskaskia Hotel

Location: La Salle, La Salle County, Illinois
Address: 217 Marquette Street, La Salle, IL 61301-2414
Phone: (815) 224-4800
Fax: (815) 224-7990
Website: www.kaskaskiahotel.com
Email: gm@KaskaskiaHotel.com or hr@KaskaskiaHotel.com

Directions: Head S towards 2nd St. and turn right on 2nd St. Then turn right on Marquette St. and you will see the hotel.

Ghost Lore

During the 1920s a young couple was spending the night in the Kaskaskia Hotel. While her boyfriend was sleeping, the woman crawled out onto the balcony of the sixth floor and dove to her death. Another version of the story states that the young woman most certainly did not commit suicide. This more sinister version tells of the boyfriend leading the woman up to the roof for a surprise. Her surprise was that he then pushed her off to her impending death below. In order to cover up his heinous murder, the boyfriend concocted a suicide story for the police. The story seemed to work, as the man was never charged and got away free, while his girlfriend is forever cursed to haunt the hotel eternally waiting for justice to be served.

- Hotel elevators seem to have a mind of their own. Employees reported getting into the elevator and pushing a button for a certain floor only to be let off at a different floor—as though a phantom hand directed a different button to be pushed.

- Many former staff believe that objects would often be moved around the hotel by some unseen force. Time and time again employees would set something down only to come back and find it missing.

- Phantom footsteps have been reported throughout the hotel. Due to the strange nature of the paranormal events, many staff get an uneasy feeling while working.

History

1912 – A group of business men from La Salle got together to form the La Salle Inn Co. It was the group's main purpose to give the people of La Salle a luxury hotel.

1913 – Construction of the hotel began. The firm of Marshall and Fox out of Chicago was chosen to design the hotel.

1915 – With much excitement in the area the hotel officially opened. The guest of honor at the event was Illinois Govenor Edward Dunne. During this time you could book a room at the hotel for only $2.50.

1927 – The hotel was being operated by Mr. and Mrs. William Hahne.

1963 – The hotel was purchased by Gildo Costa and James DeFilippi.

1965 – The Hahnes closed down the hotel and began to sell off the furniture.

1966 – The hotel was purchased by the Meade Electric Corporation out of Chicago. The original plans called for the hotel to be used as a corporate building. On second thought, the owners decided to keep the building as a hotel and end the sale of furnishings.

1975 – The Kaskaskia was sold to five businessmen.

1980 – Walter Raineri, one of the five men to purchase the building, bought out all of the other owners.

1988 – The Kaskaskia was sold to investors in California who turned the hotel into a resident hotel for seniors. The building was renamed Kensington-Kaskaskia.

1988 – The building was added to National Register of Historic Places.

1992 – The First State Bank of Mendota gained ownership of the building after foreclosing on the Kensington-Kaskaskia for an $800,000 loan. Walter and Pat Raineri took the reigns of running the senior housing building.

1998 – The building was purchased with the intent of turning it back into a full service hotel.

2001 – The hotel once again closed down.

2006 – Developer Blouke Carus released the Kaskaskia Hotel and Conference Center business plan to focus on re-opening the hotel. The cost of the renovation plan was estimated at $17 million.

Currently – Developers, investors, and La Salle's mayor are working on a renovation and re-opening project for the hotel slated for late 2008 or early 2009.

Source: *The News Tribune* – La Salle

Investigation

A suicide did take place at the Kaskaskia, but not quite in the manner of the ghost lore. Actually, the real story is much more fascinating and intriguing than the ghost lore. Enjoy the real story. On July 4th, 1948 the *Dixon Telegraph* reported that Mrs. Edward Metzger plunged to her death from the Kaskaskia Hotel. It was believed that she jumped from the sixth story rooftop. The paper reported that while Mrs. Metzger was jumping to her death, her husband was sound asleep in their fourth floor room. The police reported that a barefoot Mrs. Metzger wearing only a nightgown quietly snuck out of her room without waking her husband. The police believed that she climbed the fire escape to the roof of the hotel where she jumped to the sidewalk below. The officers investigating the case went to the Metzger's room where they found Edward Metzger sound asleep in bed. The police did find a suicide note left behind by Mrs. Metzger.

We found the death certificate stating that Mrs. Edward Metzger's official name was Norma Metzger. Further investigation revealed an article in The *Harrisburg Daily Register* on June 5, 1948. The article reported that the couple had a six-year-old daughter that was in the Springfield hospital for an operation. Mr. Metzger testified at a coroner's inquest that he had no quarrel with his wife, and he had observed her writing a note at the desk yet he was not aware of its contents. The suicide note was read at the inquest and is as follows:

"I should be too proud to admit that my own husband would not kiss me. But then I figured it must be my fault, that I am crazy. I have a persecution complex, yet the fact remains that I have to beg for love and yet not get it—from my husband. Others offer, or is it just a line? Or is it that familiarity breeds contempt—for me?"

A former employee told us that on numerous occasions while she was cleaning the sixth floor, she would hear footsteps of someone walking down the hallway. Knowing that the floor was supposed to be empty, the woman set out to find the footsteps. As soon and she went to investigate, the phantom footsteps simply stopped. Several other employees we spoke with told us similar accounts of encountering the ghostly footsteps. Many of employees refused to work alone on the sixth floor.

Many of the staff would complain that objects throughout the hotel would be moved and rearranged by the hands of some unknown spirit. Cleaning supplies, furniture, and personal items all became part of the mysterious activity.

Pointing Ghost of 23rd Avenue

Location: Moline, Rock Island County, IL

Directions: Follow 23rd Ave. The spirit is said to roam the street.

Ghost Lore

The vanishing hitchhiker is one of the most popular legends in the U.S. The phantom woman has been spotted in every state, mostly at night along dark, deserted back roads. The people of Moline also have a ghost of a woman lurking in the road, yet this one does not want a ride home. Those who pass by along 23rd Avenue often spot the spirit of an attractive woman standing on the side of the road. The woman is dressed in Victorian style clothing and at the end of her outstretched hand rests her ghostly finger that endlessly points to some unknown destination. Who or what the spirit is pointing at is unknown, but local lore tells that the spirit is a good Samaritan that only wants to help you.

- More sinister tales of the woman tell of a different purpose for the spirit. Many believe that the spirit only points at people to expose their guilt.

- Superstitious townsfolk believed that the pointing ghost was a forbearer of doom and that if she pointed at you, painful death would soon follow.

History

1836 – David Sears arrived in Rock Island Mills.

1843 – The town was platted by David B. Sears, Spencer White, Joel and Huntington Wells, Charles Atkinson, and Nathan Bass. The name Moline was said to be the French word for mill.

1844 – A post office was established in town.

1848 – The legal records of Moline being platted in 1843 were lost to fire. The town was officially incorporated.

1854 – The first train through Moline made an appearance.

1855 – Moline was reincorporated as a town.

1872 – Moline was incorporated as a city. Daniel L. Wheelock was elected as the city's first Mayor.

Source: *My Moline* by John Cervantes

Investigation

This long stretch of 23rd Avenue is made up of both residential homes and businesses.

The story of the pointing ghost was documented by Bruce Carlson in his book *Ghosts of Rock Island County*. Carlson wrote of several stories about the pointing ghost. The first legend about the ghost is the one that terrified the residents of the area. It was said that if the woman pointed at you, death would not be far behind. Her reputation for predicting death may have been tarnished when she was

155

seen pointing outside the home of a man who was deathly ill. By a stroke of luck, the man quickly recovered and lived on for many years.

The second story Carlson documented tells of the woman being spotted standing in a yard pointing at the home of a man who was about to face criminal court charges. Immediately, town speculation claimed that she only pointed at those who were guilty of a crime. Yet, once again the woman's reputation failed her when the accused man was acquitted.

The third story from Carlson shows that the pointing spirit may have a mischievous side to her. This story takes the reader back many years to a high-class social event taking place at an elegant home in Moline. Early in the festivities, one of the guests had trouble holding his drink and was a bit intoxicated when he set off in search of the restroom. As he stumbled up the stairs, he clumsily opened the first door he saw. Instead of finding the bathroom, the man had discovered the bedroom. At this point, a helpful young lady pointed him to the room directly down the hall. Giving the woman a slurred thank you, he made a rush for the bathroom to relieve himself. Unbeknownst to the drunken man, the spirit of the pointing lady had misdirected him. Instead of pointing to the restroom, the woman sent him to the balcony directly overlooking a group of prominent party attendees. Just as the man was about to commit social suicide, his friend grabbed him and escorted him back to the restroom.

Several residents of 23rd Avenue told us that while they were aware of the history of the pointing ghost, they never had a personal sighting.

As more and more homes and business moved into the area, the reports of the woman decreased.

The Dare. If you find the spirit of 23rd Avenue and get her to point at you, your death will soon follow.

Cry Baby Bridge

Location: Monmouth, Warren County, IL

Directions: As you head north to Monmouth on Hwy 67, you will see a Farm King on your right. On that road (210th) turn left. Follow this road for approximately 1 mile until you see a gravel road on your right. Take this road for 2 miles and you will reach the bridge.

Ghost Lore

Throughout the United States there are hundreds of bridges that are rumored to be haunted. In years past people believed that the dead could not cross running water. They often buried their loved ones across the river, thereby trapping them from crossing back over the water into the village. Others believe that not only do bridges connect the earth with the water, but they also metaphorically connect the living world with the spirit world. But, regardless of whether or not you believe these theories, the people of Monmouth believe the secluded bridge dubbed "cry baby bridge" may be haunted by several ghosts.

- A young couple was speeding around the curvy road way too fast, lost control of their car and drove off the bridge and died in the murky churning water of the river.

- A school bus full of playful children lost control and plunged into the river, ending the lives of all the children on board.

- The ghosts of the young children killed in an accident will push your car over the bridge to safety to ensure that you do not suffer their fate.

History

Little is known of the history of the bridge, which may add to the mystery of the area and story.

We spoke with the library, residents, and local historians, yet no information on the bridge surfaced.

Investigation

According to local lore, the stories of the bridge being haunted go back over 50 years.

Nearly everyone we spoke with in town knew of the haunted cry baby bridge story. In our research we found that several different versions of the legend exist. One version of the tale tells of a young mother who went insane and brought her young child out to the river and threw it over the side of the bridge to its watery grave. Another version told to us involves an older man who was out at the bridge fishing. This was his favorite fishing spot, and he set up his gear right off of the bridge, looking to land the big one. While he was fishing, a group of young kids came speeding by in their car and hit the old man, killing him instantly.

Two young residents told us that one evening they traveled out to the bridge to see for themselves what everyone was talking about. They had heard that if you stop your car and put it neutral, the spirits of the dead children will push your car over the bridge to safety. Following the legends directions they put their car in neutral

and sure enough, it started to move on its own. Unfortunately, they never found out who or what was pushing the car, because as soon as the car started to move, the group got scared and sped out of the area as fast as they could.

A woman related her personal experience to us. It began late one evening when the woman decided to venture out into the country to investigate the bridge. For years she had heard the stories told to her by friends, yet she remained skeptical. Shortly after the woman arrived, she heard the faint sound of a baby crying. Curious, and a little frightened, the woman scoured the area to find the baby, but after a thorough search she was unable to locate the "baby."

Another woman informed us that when she visited the bridge, she was able to hear the sounds of people crying, but again no cause for the mysterious crying could be located.

We were unable to locate any reports of deaths or accidents taking place on the bridge.

Raven's Grin Inn

Location: Mount Carroll, Carroll County, Illinois
Address: 411 North Carroll Street, Mount Carroll, IL 61053-1007
Phone: (815) 244-4746
Website: www.hauntedravensgrin.com

Directions: Head east on West Spring St. toward North Galena St. Turn right on North Galena St. and follow to North Carroll St. Follow North Carroll St. to the dead end, and you will be at the Grin Inn.

Ghost Lore

Normally we don't play favorites in our books. However, we just could not resist making an exception for the Raven's Grin Inn. Once you visit this wonderfully sinister looking home, you will see why we gave it such a high rating. The first thing you need to know about the Inn is that it is a "haunted" haunted house, meaning that when you are walking through the home, if the eerie props don't scare you, the real spirits of the house just might. At first glance, the amazing home looks like it popped out of out of Hollywood as some weird Tim Burton creation. However, when you take the tour you will quickly see that unlike Hollywood, the Inn provides a perfect combination of being both campy and creative. Although the owner has been giving people spooky tours for over 20 years, the spirits in the home have been spooking visitors for over 135 years.

- Townsfolk tell many stories of the haunted history of the building, including the ghost of a female who refuses to leave.

- Rumors state that the speakeasy located in the basement of the building was closed for business because the fear of the ghost drove off many potential customers.

- Numerous psychics have sensed that the home has several ghosts roaming its halls.

History

1870 – The home was constructed by Charles Nohe. The original purpose of the building was to serve as an inn and tavern.

1885 – The place was called Mother Nohe's. The establishment was said to be a truly wild place of fun and debauchery. It was also well-known in the area as being a house of ill repute.

1898 – A huge tornado ripped through the area. Luckily, most of the town took shelter in the security of the wine cellar in the basement of the inn.

1900 – The building was also used as a schoolhouse for local children.

1925 – The basement was a speakeasy in which many people sought refuge from prohibition. The speakeasy even had a cool secret door. (The door still remains, but you will have to find it for yourself.)

1925 – Many believed that this is when the ghostly activity began. Reports from the time period state that a female ghost was often spotted floating throughout the inn.

1930 – The building served as an Oldsmobile dealership selling cars to the community.

1970 – The home was being used for apartment rentals.

1987 – Jim Warfield and his wife bought the historical home.

1988 – Jim began guiding ghost tours though the home.

Investigation

The home does have a long and sorted history, including many cases of paranormal activity.

Many of the tales of ghostly activity seemed to leak out during the 1920s when the place was still being used as a speakeasy. During this time, many visitors would visit the inn for a drink or to partake in the "ladies of the night." Jonathan Battle wrote in his article "Haunted Hudsons," that visitors reported seeing a female ghost that would appear in a white gown on one side of the room. The spirit would float along the floor and mysteriously disappear into a vent on the other side of the room. The ghost was observed so many times by so many visitors that they gave her a name. The spirit was then known as Matilda. Up until the time the spirit made her appearance, the inn was a thriving business. Speculation among many in the community stated that the demise of the club was due to Matilda literally scaring off customers.

One day any elderly woman appeared on the inn's doorstep. She informed the owner that she was the daughter of a man who owned the building many years ago. The woman told a story that seemed to give credibility to the story of the inn's closing. The woman said that the speakeasy did indeed close because people were scared off because they feared that they might encounter Matilda.

On one of the tours, a group was exploring the old wine cellar when they spotted the spirit of a woman wearing a white dress standing in the northeast corner. The woman appeared to be about 30-35 years of age and had long dark hair. The group was amazed at the sighting and could only stare at the apparition as she shot up into the vent and disappeared.

An elderly man had just finished taking the tour and wanted to capture the moment with a picture of himself in front of the house. He jokingly said, "If there are any ghosts in this room, they'll be right here," referring to his outstretched hand. When the picture was developed, the man about fell over when he noticed a shapeless gray form hovering at the end of his arm.

Both Jim and Jessica live in the home, and Jessica has experienced several odd things while staying there. One evening she was awaken by the odd sounds of a soft cry. As she quietly listened, the sobbing continued to get louder and louder until the cries finally exploded into a piercing scream. After the scream, the sounds mysteriously stopped. What made Jessica's experience even more puzzling was the fact that both her cat and dog heard the ghostly scream.

Albino Cemetery

Location: Preemption Township, Mercer County, Illinois

Directions: From Aledo on Hwy 47 take State Hwy 94 to the north. Turn right on Ridge Rd. and go past Corn's Cemetery and follow the bend. Turn right on 230th St. and the road will come to a Y. Take a right and the cemetery will be on your right.

Ghost Lore

Of all the cases in this book, the albino cemetery is one of the least well known. It seems that much like the secluded cemetery itself, the haunted stories are only known by those who have grown up in the area. But beware, because the cemetery is said to be haunted by the angry spirits of albinos who make their home in the nearby forest. When unsuspecting visitors make their way to the cemetery, they are chased away by these phantom albinos that are hell bent on protecting the area.

Inside the cemetery sits a giant brick cross. At night if you attempt to kiss the cross phantom spirits will prevent you from doing so.

History

1835 – Hopkins Boone, a relative of Daniel Boone arrived in Preemption Township.

1837 – A post office was established in town which was thought of as the beginning of the community.

1854 – Joseph Conway purchased the land where the cemetery sits.

1860 – The census listed Joseph living with his mother, Mary, and what were presumed his brothers Michael, John, James, and possible sister Margaret. It is believed that John and James Conway passed away shortly after the census, and thus the family burial ground started. The family probably asked a priest to consecrate the cemetery ground. No date of death is listed on James' and John's gravestones. They are buried next to their brother Michael, who passed away in 1862.

1861 – Francis Curry died and was buried in the cemetery. This gravestone has the oldest listed death date in the cemetery.

1862 – Michael Conway passed away and was buried next to the grave of Curry. Next to Michael sits the grave stones of John and James Conway.

1875 – Members of the community decided that an official church building was needed. A drive for funds and materials was started and signed by the Macks, Conways, Dooleys, Lucuses, McMannies and others. Mathias Schnell was contracted and completed the church.

1875 – The cemetery, which was probably known as the Conway Cemetery, was changed to the St. Joseph's Cemetery when the St.

Joseph Church was dedicated by Father I. P. Rowles.

1875 – The St. Joseph Church was constructed on land owned by the Conway family a half mile north of the cemetery.

Source: Bill A. Bertrand

Investigation

The correct name of the cemetery is St. Joseph. It is believed that the cemetery started as a family burial ground for the Conway family. Inside the cemetery is a stone that reads "Michael Conway Buried in Ireland." Michael was the father of Joseph, John and Margaret. It is believed that Michael passed away before his family emigrated to the U.S., and the stone was erected in his memory.

A young woman told us that she ventured out to the cemetery with a few friends one evening to test the legend of the albinos. As she cautiously drove her Jeep into the cemetery, the night air seemed calm and quiet. The friends got out and hurriedly moved toward the large brick cross and kissed it. As soon as they had removed their lips from the monument, they noticed several shadowy figures emerge from the trees. Not waiting to see what the mysterious figures wanted, the frightened group rushed back to the Jeep, sped off, and didn't look back until they reached the safety of the town.

We spoke with a young woman in town who had always heard of the albino spirits that roamed the cemetery and nearby woods. Yet, this woman was a non-believer and felt that the stories were nothing more than urban legend.

The Dare. If you enter the cemetery at night and kiss the giant brick cross, the Albinos will appear and chase you off the land.

Villa de Chantal

Location: Rock Island, Rock Island County, Illinois
Address: 2000 26th Avenue, Rock Island, IL 61201

Directions: Take 20th St. up the hill and turn left on 16th Ave. The entrance will be on your left at the corner of 16th and 21st St.

Ghost Lore

Perfectly perched on top of the hillside overlooking the city sits the historic Villa de Chantal Catholic School. This imposing Gothic Revival building has provided its students and the community with over 100 years of fond memories. However, some residents believe the history of "The Villa" is not so happy. Whispers of priests impregnating nuns, multiple suicides, and buried infants makes the Villa a must-see location for those with a macabre curiosity.

- While visiting the Villa you will hear eerie knocking coming from inside the walls.

- If you venture into the old building, you will be followed by mysterious footsteps.

- The grounds are haunted by the spirits of the numerous students who have taken their own lives while attending the Villa.

History

1899 – The Visitation nuns traveled from their home in Kentucky to Rock Island in order to establish a private school for girls.

1900 – Land that served as a cow pasture known as Ball's Bluff was purchased for $11,000.

1901 – The school, which was designed by George Stauduhar, was completed.

1901 – Classes began for boarding students. The school accepted students from ages 5 to 18 to attend classes.

1906 – Due to the popularity of the school, the sisters decided to borrow $80,000 in order to construct a second wing on the building that was essential for the growing school.

1907 – A ceremony was held to dedicate the Villa Chapel.

1919 – The Chaplin's bungalow was finished.

1929 – Construction on a new classroom was started due to a grant from Frank Lewis. The new structure contained a gym, cafeteria, offices, and additional classrooms for the students.

1954 – Construction on an addition to the monastery was completed.

1958 – The boarding school closed its doors, opening up as a day school for students within the community.

1975 – The *Rock Island Argus* newspaper reported that the last class graduated from the high school.

1976 – The school's junior high closed down due to financial troubles.

1977 – The school announced that its kindergarten and grade school would be closing.

1978 – Due to financial problems, the historic school finally closed down.

1979 – The sisters leased the building to Western Illinois University, which used it as a continuing education center.

1992 – According to Richard Soseman the monastery closed.

1994 – The building was given Landmark Status.

1995 – The building was sold to Dr. Joe Seng from Davenport Iowa.

2004 – The building was purchased by Villa L.C. for $2.4 million.

2005 – The building was placed on the National Register of Historic Places.

2005 – A tragic fire destroyed much of the grounds.

2006 – According to the *Quad City Times,* Villa L.C. sued their insurance company, which had apparently refused payment on the fire damage claim.

Currently – Renovations and repairs are being made, yet the future of the building is unknown. The *Quad City Times* reports that the current owner, Chris Ales, has plans to open the building as apartments for senior living in 2007.

Investigation

Many Catholic schools of years past have had a reputation of being the home of cruel, tragic, and strange events. With over 100 years of history and thousands of students passing through its doors, you can imagine that some odd things have taken place at the Villa.

Several young residents informed us that sinister folklore about the Villa is told throughout town. One of the more fascinating tales of the Villa revolves around the nuns of the school. It is said that the nuns would often partake in sexual relationships with priests from the area. In the course of their forbidden love affair, the nuns would sometimes find themselves pregnant. With the fact that they took a vow of celibacy, along with the public outrage that would have followed, the nuns could not bring their unborn children to

life. Rumors circulated that the fetuses were aborted and disposed of in the walls of the schools.

Those who are brave enough to venture to the old building report hearing strange knocking and crying coming from the inside of the walls. These eerie noises are said to be the spirits of the babies left in the walls by the nuns.

We were unable to locate any solid evidence of nuns having babies while at the Villa. If these babies were in the walls, they may have been forever lost in the fire of 2005.

Ghostly footsteps have been reported throughout the building, even though the source of the phantom footsteps has never been found.

We were unable to locate any reports of suicides that took place at the Villa. However, many times stories of suicides at schools were not printed or have yet to be found.

Several friends went to the Villa to see if the stories of the ghosts were true. While they were walking through the building, they reported hearing a mysterious female scream, yet after much exploring the source of the eerie scream was never found.

Seventh Avenue Dead End

Location: Sterling, Whiteside County, Illinois

Directions: Take 7th Ave. towards the Rock River and you will hit the dead end.

Ghost Lore

In the unfortunate modern day pursuit of all-out homogeny, towns all across the U.S. have changed signs that once read "Dead End" to a much fluffier "No Outlet," in hopes of getting rid of the negative connotation that seems to cling to "Dead End." Even with the forced changes, many people still refer to roads with no escape as being "Dead Ends." The city of Sterling has a unique dead end, as many residents believe that this dead end is haunted by a woman eternally searching for her lost child.

- Many people have died near this "blind corner," either being hit by an oncoming train or succumbing to the waters of the Rock River.

- A mysterious figure haunts the railroad tracks looking for her children.

- Eerie noises have been reported by those who venture to the dead end.

History

1834 – Hezekiah Brink built a cabin in the area called Harrisburg.

1836 – William Kirkpatrick constructed a cabin in Chatham.

1836 – The two towns of Harrisburg and Chatham combined to make Sterling.

1857 – The town of Sterling was incorporated as a city.

Investigation

Seventh Avenue runs perpendicular to the Rock River and the dead end stops before hitting the railroad tracks.

Situated along the dead end road sit several homes. We spoke with several residents of the area regarding the strange events said to take place on the road. Those we spoke with had heard the stories but did not have any personal experiences with the ghostly activity.

We also heard several stories from residents about the ghost of a young mother who has been spotted walking along the riverbank at night. Many witnesses also report hearing the eerie wail of this woman, as she is said to eternally walk the area searching for her lost children.

Local lore tells of numerous people who have met their untimely death by drowning in the Rock River. The ghostly spirits of these unfortunate souls can be witnessed along the river banks near Seventh Avenue.

Staff at the Historical Society, along with the library's genealogy department, had not heard of the hauntings.

We were unable to get any specific names associated with the drowning or railroad ghosts. However, based on stories and obituaries from the *Sterling Daily Gazette,* hundreds of people have drowned in the Rock River throughout the years, and the same can be said for those who meet their fate at the hands of the railroad.

Headless Woman of Cumberland Cemetery

Location: Wenona, Marshall County, Illinois

Directions: From Main St. turn left on West Elm St. (900N) (right before Casey's General Store). Follow that road for approximately 2.5 miles and turn right on 2800E. You will pass a cemetery on your right. Do not turn here! Continue on down the hill and take your first left (Evans Rd.) then turn right on Cumberland Rd. and the cemetery will be straight ahead.

Ghost Lore

Years ago, before Cumberland Cemetery occupied the area, a farmer and his family grew crops on the land. It was said that the man loved both his work and his family, but it was his wife that truly held his heart. As the years passed by, it seemed that life could not get any better for the lucky young man, but they could certainly get worse. The husband began to fear that his wife was stepping out on him with another man. The very thought of his wife's betrayal burned at his soul. This pain caused him to spiral into a bout of madness where he set about to end her affair forever. While his wife was busy at work in the barn, the man picked up his freshly sharpened axe, walked toward his wife and took off her head with one mighty swipe. Her headless body fell next to a nearby stump where the cemetery now rests. Since that time the headless spirit of the woman has been seen drifting through the cemetery.

- A phantom little girl has been seen roaming the cemetery. Her spirit is trapped on the land that took her life many years ago.

- Mysterious balls of lights often hover inside the secluded cemetery. If you approach the lights, they will suddenly vanish into thin air.

History

1824 – Benjamin Darnell built his cabin on the ground.

1829 – Lucy Darnell died just short of her 13th birthday. She was the first burial on the land.

1832 – During the Black Hawk War, a stockade was built on the Darnell property. The stockade was 10 feet high and could hold and protect 100 people in the event of a Native American attack.

1875 – A public meeting was held near the Cumberland Presbyterian Church, and they formed the Cumberland Cemetery Association.

1875 – At the first meeting of the association, it was decided that an addition to the old cemetery was to be purchased. The cemetery was also set to be plotted and existing graves needed to be recorded.

1876 – Cemetery lots were sold off at auction. The lots cost around $40 a piece.

1878 – Robert Mann was put in charge of the cemetery's maintenance. His job was to purchase lumber, repair the fence, and construct boxes for use in the cemetery.

1881 – Years before Congress passed the 19th Amendment that allowed women to vote in elections, the association voted that any widow that held a deed, or widows of deceased husbands who held a deed, should be allowed to vote on cemetery matters.

1891 – Ten angry members of the cemetery association petitioned the leaders to not allow the pasture of sheep on the land.

1892 – The cost for digging a grave was increased. If the deceased was under the age of twelve, the cost for digging the grave was $3.75. Those over the age of twelve were charged $5 for the service.

1928 – An arch gate was constructed at the south entrance of the cemetery. Mrs. Wilbur Mann and Cora Dickey were duly responsible for the arch.

1942 – A vote was passed to incorporate the cemetery association.

1947 – The group was granted a Cemetery Association License. The Cumberland Cemetery Association transferred all funds, deeds, etc., to the new Evans Township Cumberland Cemetery Association of Wenona, Illinois.

1956 – The cemetery arch was widened to accommodate the wider vehicles of the time.

1963 – Over 200 people attended the William Hunt Tree Dedication. The tree had been planted to protect the body of William Hunt. It was common practice during this time period for freshly buried bodies to be dug up and sold to medical colleges.

Source: *Old Sandy Remembers* by the Marshall County Historical Society

Investigation

Many witnesses have reported seeing the ghost of a little girl inside the cemetery. When those lucky enough to spot her try to get closer, she simply disappears into thin air. This tale seems to be centered around the first burial to have taken place on the land where the cemetery now rests. In 1829, a young girl named Lucy Darnell died just before her 13th birthday. Lucy had the honor of being the first person buried on the land. Years later in 1880, the *Henry Republican* published a short piece on the burial of Lucy. The article stated that Lucy had suddenly fallen ill and passed away. Her coffin was built by chopping down a walnut tree and splitting out a few slabs. The pieces were put together to form a homemade coffin. According to those present, the coffin looked very respectable.

Often visitors to the cemetery report seeing the ghostly apparition of a headless woman drifting through the cemetery. The mysterious woman has also been sighted by those driving by the old cemetery. Everyone who sees her reports that she is indeed without a head.

We were unable to find any evidence of a woman being murdered by her jealous husband. In the early 1820s, Benjamin Darnell built a cabin on the land where he lived with his wife and their children James, Larkin, Enoch, Benjamin, and Lucy. We were unable to find any evidence that Mrs. Darnell was ever murdered.

The story of the cemetery being haunted has been told for many generations. We spoke with a few residents that told us that when they were kids in the 1950s they recalled hearing stories about the haunted cemetery.

We were told by several residents that the cemetery is filled with vaporous balls of light that dance their way through the cemetery. On one occasion two friends were bored and they thought that a trip out to the secluded haunted cemetery would spark up their evening. Having heard of the cemetery's haunted reputation, the friends kept their eyes open, hoping to catch a glimpse of the headless ghost as they slowly approached the graveyard.

After spending the better part of an hour walking through the cemetery, the friends decided to pack it up and call it a night. Just as they were heading back for their car, they noticed a small ball of white light moving around on the outskirts of the cemetery. Curious as to what the light actually was, they moved forward to get a better view. As they got closer the light seemed to increase in size and change color. Convinced that someone was playing a trick on them, the friends moved even closer to the light. As they were stealthily creeping towards the light, it disappeared into thin air. The two friends left the cemetery thoroughly convinced that the it was haunted.

SOUTHERN ILLINOIS

Elijah P. Lovejoy Monument

Location: Alton, Madison County, Illinois
Address: Monument Avenue, Alton, IL 62002

Directions: Take Broadway St to the west. From there, turn right on Monument Ave. and it will lead you to the Lovejoy Monument.

Ghost Lore

Today in the U.S. you often see signs and bumper stickers with the saying, "Freedom isn't free." Unfortunately, the saying rings true when it comes to our country's past as evidenced by the disheartening tale of Elijah Lovejoy. In the days of human slavery in the U.S., Elijah Lovejoy used his position as a newspaper editor to speak out on the evils of slavery. Ultimately these progressive views would cost Lovejoy his life. Many years later, Lovejoy's words and ideals are celebrated and honored by thousands of visitors who pay their respect while at his grave. For many, the words of Elijah Lovejoy will never die, yet for other unsuspecting visitors it is his spirit that refuses to die.

- For many years, the ghost image of a man has been seem walking the grounds of Lovejoy's grave.

- Unexplained cold drafts slowly float through the cemetery.

History

1802 – Elijah Parish Lovejoy was born in the town of Albion Maine.

1826 – Lovejoy graduated from Waterville College (now known as Colby College).

1834 – Lovejoy served as a pastor for a Presbyterian Church in St. Louis. It was here that he started a religious newspaper with the focus on elimination of slavery.

1837 – Lovejoy was shot dead while trying to protect a new printer from an angry mob of white slave-owners.

1850s – The idea was formed to place a memorial to Lovejoy in the entrance of the new cemetery.

1856 – An architect named J. A. Miller was hired to design the monument.

1886 – A Lovejoy Monument Association was formed.

1897 – The Lovejoy Monument was officially dedicated.

Investigation

The story of Elijah Lovejoy is both courageous and tragic. In 1937, the Alton Observer reported that Lovejoy and approximately 20 of his supporters were gathered in an old warehouse. These brave men were on a mission to protect a new printing press that had been delivered to Lovejoy. An angry mob of white slave-owners, dis-

pleased with Loveyjoy's anti-slavery writings, had gathered outside. The mob had come to the office with the unified goal of destroying Lovejoy's new press in hopes that it would prevent him from spreading the anti-slavery message.

As darkness grew, the mob became impatient and started throwing rocks and stones into the three story building where the men were held up. The men inside retaliated by throwing what ever materials they could find inside the building. Eventually the mob started firing into the building, and return fire was immediate. A young boy was sent up a ladder with the intent of starting the roof on fire. His plan was thwarted when the ladder was pushed back from the building by the men. However, the young boy tried again. This time when Lovejoy went to push the ladder away, he was spotted and gunfire rang out. Lovejoy was hit five times and died almost

instantaneously. With the roof catching fire the remaining men inside had no choice but to lay down their weapons and leave. The printing press was torn apart and thrown into the Mississippi River to meet its watery grave. The next morning Lovejoy's body was removed from the building and given a burial.

Since Lovejoy's death, many people have reported seeing the ghostly image of a man walking the grounds near the grave of Elijah Lovejoy. Many believed that the ghost was that of Lovejoy himself who refused to rest in peace.

We spoke with several cemetery employees who told us several other legends of the cemetery. Although the men did not believe in ghost themselves, they reported that many visitors to the Lovejoy Monument have reported feeling a cold draft pass through even on the hottest days of the year. They also have heard stories of the cemetery being haunted by the restless ghost of Lovejoy.

Others believe that the cemetery is haunted by the ghost of a young girl who has been spotted moving throughout the grounds. We were unable to confirm the story of the ghostly little girl.

Currently many of the ghost tours of Alton make a stop at the monument to give tourgoers a chance to come face to face with Elijah Lovejoy's ghost.

McPike Mansion

Location: Alton, Madison County, Illinois
AKA: Mount Lookout
Address: 2018 Alby Street, Alton, IL 62002-6814
Phone: (618) 462-3348
Email: mcpikemansion@charter.net
Website: www.mcpikemansion.com

Directions: Take Piasa St. to the north. Turn right on W 9th St. Turn left on Alby St., and the mansion will be up a few blocks on your left.

Ghost Lore

When driving past the homes of this residential neighborhood, you certainly do not expect to find the historic McPike Mansion. The grand mansion is perched on the corner of the block overlooking the city. Yet, when you approach the yard and first set eyes on the mansion, it is impossible not to be whisked back to a time when the home was in its glory days. You can almost hear the children playing games in the large lush backyard; you can taste the cool lemonade the women are sipping in the shade offered by the lovely front porch. Any minute you expect to see Henry McPike walk out of the main door, offering you a cigar and a chat. The picture in your mind is so perfect that you are convinced that no one would want to leave. Well, you may be right, as the current owners believe the place has several former workers and residents that refuse to leave, even after their death.

- Although the home is currently empty, unknown figures have been seen peaking out of the windows.

- Photographs of the mansion often reveal strange paranormal activity that was not present to the naked eye.

- Unknown bodies are buried on the grounds in the backyard of the mansion.

- During the years when the house sat empty, many in the community referred to it as the "old haunted house." Little did they know how right they were.

History

According to the owners many of the dates of the history of the home are fuzzy.

1869 – The home was constructed on the wishes of Henry Guest McPike by the architect Lucas Pfeiffenberger in a fabulous Italianate-Victorian style.

1908 – Many believe that Paul Laichinger purchased the home during this time period. Others believe that the McPike family continued to live in the home.

1936 – Some believe that the McPike mansion, which had been occupied by McPike family members, was sold to Paul Laichinger. Mr. Laichinger rented the home out to various borders.

1950 – The once majestic house was dilapidated, vacant, and in major need of restoration.

1980 – The home was listed on the National Register of Historic Places.

1994 – The mansion was purchased by Sharyn and George Luedke at an auction.

1998 – The home was listed as one of Illinois' "Ten Most Endangered Historic Places" by the Landmarks Preservation Council of Illinois.

2001 – The Alton City Council voted 4 to 3 to amend the city's trespassing ordinance which allowed the McPike Mansion to continue with their "Haunted Halloween" gathering.

Currently – The mansion is slowly being restored by the Ludkes.

Investigation

Those who rented rooms in the house during the 1940s told odd stories of parents that would often yell at their children for continuously running up and down the staircase. However, when the running noises did not cease, the parent, convinced that the child did not heed their warning, went to discipline the child only to find that the stairs were empty; the only thing that remained was the lingering noise of the phantom feet.

Visitors to the historic mansion often spend time walking around the outside of the home taking in its history. While enjoying their leisurely stroll, visitors are surprised when they see mysterious faces peeking out of the windows. The visitors are even further surprised when they find out that no one is occupying the home.

According to *The Telegraph* newspaper, in 1976, while visiting the home, Antoinette Eason, a psychic, and a friend were looking at the home when they saw a third story window open by itself.

One of the most reported spirits of the house is that of a young female spirit that witnesses have dubbed "Sarah." Sarah has been known to touch, hug, and playfully pinch those who visit to the mansion. It is believed that Sarah once worked in the mansion as a servant.

Even though Paul Laichinger died many years ago, witnesses still report seeing the former owner walking around the mansion. It is believed that his spirit is continuing to do maintenance on the home, much as he did while he was alive. It appears that even from the afterlife, he is keeping a close eye on his old home.

Strange noises have been heard inside the home, including the sounds of people talking when no one is around and mysterious footsteps that can be heard and not seen.

The mansion is also home to many mysterious scents. Visitors have reported catching the scent of lilac during the winter, and, even though smoking was not allowed inside the home, guests report smelling phantom cigarette smoke throughout the house.

Numerous people have taken pictures of the mansion. When they got the film developed (or looked at the digital), they are amazed to find that something that was not there to the naked eye when the photo was taken appears on the photo. Oftentimes these visitors captured strange orbs, outlines of figures standing in the windows, and unusual glowing eyes on their film. Make sure you ask the owner to show you all the paranormal photos that have been taken at the mansion.

The owner believes that several unknown bodies are buried in the backyard of the house. It is believed that these bodies are buried on the haunted trail that runs through the land.

In addition to human spirits, the owner told us that many people believe that the mansion is home to two phantom dogs that haunt the place. These mysterious dogs have been seen and heard patrolling the grounds of the mansion.

Haunted Ghost Tracks

Location: Rentchler Station Road, Belleville, Saint Clair County, Illinois

Directions: Take 177 East from Belleville, and then turn right on 2020E (Rentchler Rd.). Keep going straight until you can not go straight any more. Here you will come to a T in the road. Follow Rentchler to the right until you reach a valley in the road. At the bottom of the valley are two orange warning signs that mark the area where the train tracks once came in on each side.

Ghost Lore

Railroad lore is very prominent in the United States. Today we seem to have forgotten just how much of an impact the railroad had on earlier life. Towns were built or deserted, fortunes acquired or lost, lives and society forever changed based simply on the path of the railroad. In Mascoutah sits an old set of railroad tracks. These tracks have a lore of their own, as many visitors to the tracks believe that they are haunted by two children, a brother and sister, who died near them.

- If you put your vehicle in neutral, the caring spirits of the young children will push your car to safety helping you avoid the fate they suffered.

- The mysterious sound of a man's voice talking can be heard when no one else is around.

History

1837 – The town of Mascoutah was established.

1850 – The Louisville & Nashville (L&N) Railroad was created through a charter by the Commonwealth of Kentucky.

1855 – The founding members of the L&N had raised nearly $3

million to finance the construction. The first train traveled eight miles with over 300 passengers.

1859 – The first train operated from Louisville to Nashville. The total cost of the construction that made the feat possible was $7,221,204.91.

1861 – The L&N Railroad had over 269 miles of track in place.

1880s – The L&N Railroad grew into one of the nation's largest railroad systems.

1909 – L&N acquired two smaller railroad lines to expand their reach.

1957 – The last steam locomotive was retired.

1969 – L&N acquired a large portion of the Chicago & Eastern Illinois Railroad which allowed it to enter the Midwest.

1971 – L&N trains ran on more than 6,574 miles of track in thirteen states.

1982 – L&N Railroad merged into the Seaboard System Railroad.

1986 – The Seaboard System became CSX Transportation.

1995-2000 – The tracks had not been used by trains in many years. The tracks were to be used as the rails to trails program. However, the land was deeded back to the original families that owned the land, and they were not in favor of the rails to trails program. The tracks were thought to have been removed at this time.

Source: *A Brief History of The Louisville & Nashville Railroad* by Charles B. Castner.

Investigation

Many of the residents know the place as "The ghost tracks," however you may have had a hard time finding this place because nearly every website lists the street as being "Renschler" when the correct name is "Rentchler."

Various stories about the tracks and the paranormal activity surrounding them have been around since at least the 1940s and perhaps much longer.

The railroad tracks that the lore is based on were the tracks of the L&N railroad. Unfortunately, the railroad tracks are no longer there. Even though the tracks have been removed, you can still see where the mighty trains once ran though the area.

The ghost tracks are also known as the Albino tracks due to a local legend. Troy Taylor wrote of this legend in his book *Weird Illinois*. Taylor wrote that two albino twins lived in the area during the late 1880s. The townsfolk believed that the unlucky albino children were contagious and would spread their disease throughout the town. The only surefire way to protect the town from a certain outbreak was to dispose of the children. Against their will, the twins were brought down to the railroad line where they were tied to the track. There they were forced to wait for the train to come steaming by and hand them their gruesome fate.

Another version of the ghost lore states that it was not a pair of twins that died at the tracks—it was a local man and his young son who were killed by the train in a tragic accident.

Locals tell the tale that if you stop your vehicle along the road where the tracks once ran and put it in neutral, you car will be mysteriously pushed over the track by unseen hands. We spoke with a woman who believes that the spirits of dead children killed on the tracks will push your vehicle back along the road because they want you to stay and play with them for awhile.

A young man told us his personal experience when he visited the ghost tracks. Bored one night, he and his friends decided to travel out to the ghost tracks to see whether the stories of it being haunted were true. Determined to get to the truth, the group stopped their car on the tracks and got out and sprinkled baby powder all over the trunk and bumper of the car. The group then got back inside the car, put it in neutral, and sat there in complete silence as their car began to move on its own. Once the vehicle stopped moving the group quickly got out of the car and were amazed to find several small hand prints pushed in the powder they had sprinkled on their car.

Washington Street Grille

Location: Belleville, Saint Clair County, Illinois
Address: 318 East Washington Street, Belleville, IL 62220-2210
Phone: (618) 239-9529
Fax: (314) 647-1056
Email: info@washingtonstreetgrille.com
Website: www.washingtonstreetgrille.com

Ghost Lore

Today, the beautiful Washington Street Grille occupies the building on East Washington Street. The welcoming building stands proud, offering visitors a chance to step back in time while enjoying a hearty meal. Many unsuspecting visitors are unaware that the building has a long history of tragedy and death. Years ago, the building was a hotel that catered to its traveling clientele. While staying at the hotel, a young family was murdered. Now many years later the vengeful spirits of that family still continue to haunt the building, eternally seeking justice for the murder.

- Screams of the mother and child can be heard while visiting the restaurant.

- The ghost of an old schoolteacher filled with guilt continues to roam the building looking for forgiveness.

History

The land was originally purchased by Mr. George Blair.

1852 – Samuel Stookey built the home to be used as his private residence.

1863 – Hanna Stookey, Samuel's daughter, married Enoch Primm. Hanna's father gave the couple the house as a wedding gift.

1904 – The home was remodeled to become the Evangelical Zion Lutheran Grade School.

1952 – The grade school closed down for good.

1956 – The structure was in rough shape and once again renovated. Robert Kelce, Jack Sauer, and Charles King turned the building into a lavish French eatery, named the Carriage House Inn.

1974 – The restaurant changed its name to The Belleville House.

1980 – The Belleville House was changed to the Pasta House.

2004 – Joy and Rob Marino renovated the restaurant and opened it as the Washington Street Grille.

2007 – February. The restaurant abruptly closed down without warning.

We are confident that another restaurant will move into the building.

Investigation

The building was never used as a hotel. However, the ghost lore is partially correct. Back when the building was a schoolhouse, local lore tells of a young boy who was playing inside the building when he accidentally tripped, fell down some stairs, and died. The headmistress at the time was a woman by the name of Effie. She believed that it was her job to protect the students, and that by failing to do so, she was ultimately responsible for the tragic death of the young boy. Overcome with guilt, Effie gathered a rope, walked to the staircase and hung herself. Her lifeless body was found dangling over the same staircase where the young boy had died.

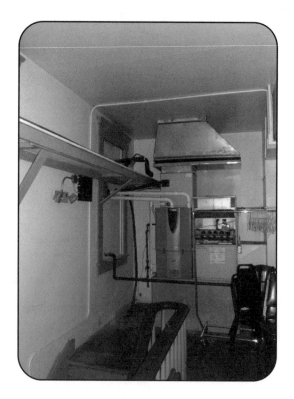

The *Belleville News Democrat* reported that Pasta House workers were in the restaurant when they heard the sounds of a dinner party going on. The workers were baffled, because the restaurant was closed, and no one else was in the building.

Other employees report that photographs hanging in the restaurant will mysteriously fly off the wall, as though they were thrown by some unseen force.

Although the owners of the Washington Street Grille believe the ghost only exists in the memories of past owners and workers, a lot of paranormal activity continues to take place.

A female employee had just finished closing up the restaurant one evening when she sat down in the kitchen to watch TV. As she sat there, she was startled by the sound of a mixing tin that fell to the floor. She got up to pick up he tin and looked over to where the noise was heard, but, much to her surprise, no tin had fallen. A bit puzzled, she thought she must have been hearing things and went to sit back down. Just as she sat back down, the lights suddenly shut off and quickly came back on.

The woman was certainly not alone in her experience. We were told that the phenomenon of lights turning on and off at the restaurant was a common experience.

Many of the employees told us that while working during the night, they often hear strange noises throughout the building. What scares the employees is the fact that the source of these phantom noises can never be located.

Violin Annie of Elmwood Cemetery

Location: Centralia, Marion County, Illinois
Correction: Some erroneously believe the cemetery is located in Central City instead of Centralia.

Directions: From N Poplar St., turn left onto Gragg St. This will lead you to the cemetery on your right.

Ghost Lore

In the small town of Centralia sits the quiet unassuming Elmwood Cemetery. At first glance the cemetery appears to be your standard run of the mill burial ground. Filled with majestic trees, old gravestones, and numerous floral arrangements, nothing out of the ordinary stands out. Yet, those who venture through the cemetery at night report a much different story, as they hear the soft sounds of a violin being played. Locals believe that the source of this mysterious music is a girl by the name of Violin Annie. The only problem with Violin Annie playing music in the cemetery is the fact that she has been dead for over 115 years. Annie suffered a horrific beating by her mother, which resulted in the young girl's death.

- If you visit the cemetery late at night on a quite evening and listen carefully, your ears will be treated to the phantom sounds of a violin.
- Each year on Halloween, Annie's monument will light up the cemetery with a mysterious glow.

History

1849 – W. Scott Marshall was born.

1860 – The first land was acquired by the city to be used as the City Cemetery. The land deed was given to the city by John G. Stevens, Theonosia W. Stevens and his wife, and Charles Floyd and Isabella Jones.

1875 – Edward Bennet Marshall was the first child born to Dr. Winfield and Eoline Marshall. Throughout much of his life, Edward was known as E. B.

1877 – The city acquired another 9 ¼ acres of land to be used for an addition to the cemetery.

1879 – Harriet Annie Marshall was born on September 7th. She was the second child of the family. It is said that Annie possessed a special gift for playing the violin.

1890 – Annie passed shortly after her 11th birthday. Death was caused by an illness that unfortunately was not recorded.

1891 – After Annie's death, an artist was commissioned to create a

large eight-foot square oil painting of Annie and her brother, E. B. In 1993, at the Albert Scott Marshall estate sale, the oil painting was purchased by Jeff Auxier.

1892 – Doctor Marshall and his wife moved to Chicago after the death of Annie.

1910 – Annie's mother, Eoline Marshall, passed away.

1921 – The name of the cemetery was changed to Elmwood Cemetery.

1922 – Doctor Marshall passed away.

1955 – Annie's brother, E. B. Marshall, passed away.

Investigation

The gravestone monument is often referred to as "A Symbol of Undying Love." The story of Annie haunting the cemetery is so prevalent in the area, it even appears on the promotional materials used for the cemetery.

The stone likeness of Annie holding her violin bears much resemblance to the oil painting that was painted of her image in 1891.

Annie was not beaten to death by her mother, as some legends say.

Some researchers believe that Annie was a child prodigy and possessed a wonderful talent for playing the violin. Reporter Wilfred Pennington found an 1890 newspaper account from the *Sentinel*

that seems to support the idea of Annie being a gifted child. It reads:

> The funeral of little Annie Marshall was held at the family residence this afternoon, conducted by Dr. J. L. Wallar; and was largely attended. Annie Marshall was a child with an unusually bright mind, and her demise is not only a sad blow to her family, but to the community as well, as she was the idol of her companions. The heart-broken parents have the sympathy of the entire city and community. The floral pieces were numerous and beautiful.

A well-used violin case was purchased from the estate of Albert Scott Marshall. The violin case was thought to have belonged to

Annie, but, unfortunately, the case did not contain her violin. What happened to Annie's violin still remains a mystery.

On quiet nights, those who are brave enough to visit the cemetery often report hearing the phantom sounds of a violin being played. This otherworldly music is believed to originate from the statue of Annie.

We spoke with a woman who passed through the cemetery on several occasions during her evening walks. On many of those walks, the woman heard the drifting sounds of a violin being played. However, the young lady did not stick around to find out where the music was coming from.

A local resident informed us that many people hold the belief that if you visit Annie's grave on Halloween night, you will see her statue eerily glowing in the dark cemetery.

We spoke with several witnesses who went to the cemetery to investigate her violin noise. While they were at the gravestone of Annie, they did not hear any music; however, what did startle them was the fact that they saw what appeared to be green tears oozing from the eyes of Annie's statue.

Gates of Hell

Location: Collinsville, Madison County, Illinois

Directions: Take Main Street to Lebanon St. There will be several tunnels or "gates of hell" along Lebanon St.

Ghost Lore

Remember the movie *The Ninth Gate* with Johnny Depp? In the film, Depp's character starts out on a dangerous quest to discover the validity of an alleged gate that would lead him to the underworld. The movie ends with the character walking towards what we are to believe is a real portal to hell. Only in Hollywood would you find a gate to hell . . . well that may not be true, especially if you live near Collinsville.

- Disbelievers that are foolish enough to drive through the tunnels off Lebanon Street will be transported to hell.

- Phantom hell hounds patrol the area while doing the Devil's bidding.

- Mysterious phantom shadows have been spotted roaming the area of the gates.

History

Much of the history of the tunnels is unknown, which certainly adds to the mysterious nature of the area.

There are seven tunnels along side the road. Some are simple railroad underpasses, while others are much more difficult to find.

Investigation

Stories of strange and unusual events taking place near the tunnels have been circulating the community for over 40 years. In 2006, Jennifer Kapiolani Saxton wrote an article for the *Belleville News-Democrat* stating that residents of Collinsville have been visiting the area of the gates for many years in search of the infamous portal to the dark world.

There are two main versions as to how you can open up the gates to hell. The first version requires you to drive through all the gates while timing it so you enter the last gate at midnight. Once under the gate, you turn off your car and wait for the witching hour to strike, and when it does you will be sucked from your car while your body and soul are transported to hell. In the second version, in order for you to get a one-way ticket to hades, you are required to pass through all seven tunnels without driving through any of them twice.

One of the main legends of the gates revolves around the mysterious devil dogs or hell hounds that are said to patrol the area. We spoke with several people who had heard that the hell hounds trot around the area looking to collect the souls of anyone who stops underneath the tunnels. Often these "dogs" are said to be dark black in color with glowing red or green eyes. Many witnesses report that the grotesque creatures are nearly transparent and often times vanish into thin air. In addition to seeing the image of the devil dogs, visitors often report hearing the faint supernatural howls of the dogs just off in the distance. Further evidence of the devil dogs come in the mysterious sound of dog chains moving through the woods as though attached to someone or something. Yet upon closer inspection, the source of this nocturnal rattling can not be found.

We spoke with several residents of the area who were familiar with stories surrounding the gates to hell. Many of them had personally ventured out to the gates in order to locate the portal. Other more daring visitors hope to stand toe to paw with a real hell hound. However, many of the visitors reported that while out in the area they could sense a presence of something unseen and were overcome with an intense fear. Many others who have been out to the gates get so scared they immediately return to town vowing to never set foot near the gates again.

The Dare. If you drive through all the tunnels before midnight and stop under the last tunnel, the earth will open up and swallow you, and your body and soul will be dragged down to hell.

Historic Miner's Institute

Location: Collinsville, Madison County, Illinois
Address: 204 West Main Street, Collinsville, IL 62234-3016
Phone: (618) 344-0026
Email: info@minersinstitute.org
Website: www.minersinstitute.org

Ghost Lore

In the mid-1800s the town of Collinsville established itself as a hotbed for mining. During the height of mining in the area, it was said that a miner could walk the entire length of the town through the numerous maze of underground tunnels running beneath the streets. The miners were responsible for constructing the beautiful Miners' Institute Building in town. Although nearly all of the mines have closed down, and the miners from the area are long gone, their memory continues to live on in their building.

However, visitors to the Miner's Building believe that more than just their memory lives on in the haunted building.

- The spirits of victims who died in the theater during the flu pandemic of the early 1900s continue to haunt the historic building.

- During the 1920s, a young actress got caught up with an unsavory gangster. The woman was in the theater when she "accidentally" fell from the rafters and died. Her ghostly spirit has been spotted floating through the theater while her unearthly voice has echoed inside the theater.

- Visitors to the theatre have reported seeing small balls of varying colored light floating through the historic building.

History

1857 – The first coal mine opened in Collinsville.

1916 – A member of the United Mine Workers convinced miners working in the area to construct a union hall and public theater.

1917 – The building was constructed at a cost of $90,000. The main source of funding was raised through the miners' union dues. Each miner had donated 1% of his salary for one year to pay for the costs of the construction of the building. The building was used for union headquarters and meetings.

1918 – The majestic building opened to the public. The cost at the time was said to have risen to $138,000.

1930 – Slowly coal mines throughout the area started to close down.

1964 – The last of the coal mines shut down in Collinsville. The remaining miners left Collinsville in search of mine work elsewhere.

1969 – The Bloomer Amusement Company purchased the building from the last remaining miners in the area. The building was used as a movie house.

1984 – The theater was closed down. The advent of multi-screen theaters and video stories were cited as the main reason for the closing.

1985 – The building was placed on the National Register of Historic Places by the State of Illinois and the U.S. Department of Interior.

1989 – The building was sold to the Miner's Institute Foundation.

1990 – Live theater was re-introduced to the building. The group,Miners Players put on the play *Our Town*.

1991 – The Miner's Institute constructed the Wall of Honor dedicated to the miners who worked in the local mines.

1993 – The building received the Historic Landmark Award.

1996 – The building underwent another renovation with the addition of new theatre seats. The inside of the theatre was also repainted.

Source: Charles Dow - Miners Institute Foundation

Investigation

There are three main stories to explain the haunted events that have occurred at the theater. Each story is complete with a unique past, death, love, and an unwillingness to leave the theater.

1. Spirits of Those Who Met Their Death In the Theatre

We spoke with a former volunteer and member of the Board of Directors for the building who informed us that the theater had a haunted reputation even before it ever opened. Shortly before the theater was slated to open, Collinsville was struck with an about of influenza. In order to prevent an even greater outbreak of the flu and to provide residents with the best care possible, many of the infected were brought to the theater for care. Unfortunately many residents succumbed to the illness and passed away inside the theater. Once the threat had diminished, the Miner's Theater did open to the public, yet since its opening day the theater was plagued with the reputation of housing the spirits of those whose lives were lost inside the theater's walls.

During a rehearsal a play group left the stage for a moment, and when they promptly returned the baby grand piano had inexplicably moved across the entire length of the stage on its own.

Other performers, while rehearsing, have seen phantom people sitting in the theater's chairs even though the theater is empty.

We spoke with an employee of a pet shop that occupies the space connected to the theater. The employee told us that oftentimes while she is working, she will hear odd noises coming from next door. She has reported hearing the sound of objects moving and voices talking in the empty building. What puzzles her about the noises is the fact that they occur when the theatre is supposed to be closed and empty.

2. The Miner Who Refuses to Leave the Theater

Locals tell the tale of a local miner believed to be named Alfred Bailey. Although much is unknown about Alfred, it is believed that he served as one of the two men who posed for the carving that sits on top of the entrance. (Alfred is the one with the mustache.) Alfred was a miner in town who loved the theater and volunteered much of his free time there. Once he retired from mining, Alfred stayed on at the theater as a handyman. We were able to find the death record of an Albert Bailey who died in Madison County on September 5, 1949. After Alfred's death, many connected with the theater believed that the paranormal happenings were connected with Alfred, who had simply chosen to continue his duties from the afterlife.

It appears that Alfred is a helpful spirit. Many workers at the theater will be searching for an item when they hear a mysterious voice tell them where to check. Once they check the area, the object is found.

It is alleged that a group of ghost investigators captured a voice on tape (EVP) saying "I am Alfred."

Many unsuspecting visitors have entered the theater for a show when they see the ghostly figure that seems to be doing maintenance on some equipment. The man is usually said to look as though he is from the early 1900s.

3. The Actress Who Is Seeking Fame and Fortune

During the 1920s a young actress at the theatre dreamed of making it big. She wanted to become a rich and famous star of the stage. Clouded by her delusions of fame and fortune, the actress hooked up with a well-known Collinsville gangster. At the time Collinsville had a number of shady characters running gambling dens, speakeasies, and brothels, so her choice of companionship wasn't viewed as being too strange. Plus, the boyfriend would often shower her with elaborate bouquets of flowers at the theater. The story goes that the woman and her boyfriend went into the theater together to have a discussion, and he was the only one to walk out. Apparently, while in the theater, the woman "accidentally" fell from the rafters. History has forgotten whether the woman died in the theater or if she died in the hospital. However, since that time her ghost has been seen haunting the theater still waiting for her big break.

A few days before each production the staff will smell the phantom scent of flowers. Although no actual flowers can be found, the scent lingers throughout the entire theater.

Several staff have encountered the ghost of a young woman while working at the theater. Often times the staff are spooked by the fact that the ghostly woman seems to interact with them.

The Dare. If you do not leave a bouquet of flowers for the ghost of the young actress on opening night, your production will be plagued with mishaps and accidents.

Three Mile House

Location: Edwardsville, Madison County, Illinois

Directions: Take Main St. N to Route 159 N. Follow for three miles. At the three mile mark, on your left hand side, you will see a large mound at the end of Miller Frontage Rd.; this is where the home once was. You will also see a large metal pole sticking out of the ground to guide you to the right spot.

Ghost Lore

During the 1800s, the Three Mile House offered the weary road traveler passing by on Route 112 some friendly hospitality, good food, and a chance to rest their tired horses before continuing on their journey. It wasn't long before the tales of the lavish and extravagant parties hosted by the house had spread throughout the region. During prohibition, the business had taken on the reputation of being a place where you could drop in for an exciting, albeit illegal, time. Filled with gambling, drinking, and prostitution, the place had a lot of secrets to hide. Yet, perhaps the most guarded secrets were the tales of paranormal activity that plagued the place.

- A former slave who died on the land was buried without ceremony and continues to walk the land waiting for his long overdue proper burial.

- President Lincoln spent the night at the inn while he made his way through the area.

- Guests to the home often encounter ghostly figures, moving chairs, and mysterious noises.

History

1852 – The 70-acre parcel of land owned by John Deterding was purchased by Frederich Gaertner for the sum of $1,200. Gaertner was a barber from St. Louis and was looking to start a new life.

1858 – Gaertner decided to invest his savings into the construction of the building that he intended to use as a roadside tavern and inn.

1863 – The tavern opened and was quickly considered the "place to be" at the time. Wealthy travelers on route out east would often spend several days enjoying the festivities of the tavern and inn.

1860s – Business was so good that Gaertner built an addition to the home. The first floor addition included a dining room, kitchen, tavern, grocery store, and a post office. The second floor was filled with 10-15 sleeping rooms.

1880s – Due to the railroad, there was a steady decline in the number of road travelers and Gaertner's business suffered. The building also suffered, as maintenance on the building was often overlooked.

1880s – When business to the inn continued to get worse, Gaertner decided to close the doors on the inn and move back to his home town of Pittsburg, Pennsylvania.

1880s-1890s – The building sat empty for many years. During this time it continued to fall into disrepair.

1900s – With the death of Frederick, the property was transferred to his son Tony.

1900s – Tony decided to sell the land to Orrie Dunlap. What Tony did not know was that Dunlap had landed several lucrative contracts from the state to build and pave Route 112. The repaving would certainly increase traffic along the road.

Throughout years the building switched owners quite frequently. Roy Mohrman, Mailey Penetoro, and the McMillan family were several of the owners.

1970 – The property was purchased by Merrill Ottwein. Ottwein was a land developer who had the grand dream of re-opening the house and returning it to its original glory. Like so many others, Ottwein never realized this dream and the building once again sat empty watching time pass by.

1975 – The building was purchased by Doug and Beverly Elliot. The Elliots immediately took to renovating the place. They had managed to transform much of the building with the goal of re-opening it for business.

1976 – The grand re-opening of the Three Mile House was held.

1982 – John Henkhaus purchased the restaurant. Henkhaus also made numerous renovations to the building, yet he too tired of the never-ending work and sold the home to back to the Elliot family.

1985 – A monstrous fire destroyed the historic home. Vigilant fire-fighters fought with the brutal flames for over five hours and had to have over 100,000 additional gallons of water shipped to the site.

Currently – The building is no longer standing, yet a small mound where the workers plowed all the remaining dirt from the home will guide you to the old spot of the Three Mile House.

Source: *Edwardsville Journal*

Investigation

The notion that Lincoln ever visited the home has been debunked by many historians including the Madison County Historical Society. We spoke with a couple of volunteers of the society that informed us that is widely believed that President Lincoln did not spend the night in Edwardsville or Madison County. Further evidence shows that even if Lincoln had decided to stay in Edwardsville, the Three Mile House would not have been his choice, as it was said that several of his close friends lived in the area, and he would have certainly spent the night at their home.

We spoke with a woman who used to go to the restaurant with her parents when she was just a child. She remembers the stories being told at that time about disembodied voices that could be heard coming from the basement.

Past visitors to the restaurant informed us that much of the town had heard stories of the haunting from the staff. It seemed the restaurant reported that many times the dining room chairs could be seen moving as though being pushed by some unseen force. Dishes would constantly rattle and fall from tables. The cause of these mysterious events was simply chalked up to the spirits haunting the building.

Researcher Troy Taylor reported that often times at night, the Elliot family would see small balls of flickering light dancing throughout their home. Taylor also found that the young daughter, Lynn Elliot, felt that dark shadows would visit her and chase her around her bedroom.

The local lore also tells that the home is haunted by the spirit of an angry slave that is unable to rest. The story tells of a slave that passed away while working on the land. The slave's remains were buried, but he was not given a proper Christian burial. Without having the proper burial, the spirit of the slave is forced to wander the land anxiously awaiting his eternal freedom. In 1983, the *Edwardsville Journal* published an article that shed some light on the slave lore. The paper reported that Henkhaus (former owner) was often visited by clergymen, and laypersons that had set out with the goal of discovering the slave's grave. Countless holes were dug in and around the basement of the home, yet the body of the slave remained hidden.

The *Edwardsville Journal* also reported that KMOX radio visited the site for a Halloween broadcast. With them were several ghost investigators intent on finding the elusive gravesite. Like so many others in the past, they too failed to uncover the burial ground. However, through a séance and Ouija board, they claimed to have contacted the spirit of the slave buried on the land. The slave's name was said to be Tom.

Unfortunately the home succumbed to fire. According to the *Edwardsville Intelligencer*, the fire was believed to have been started in the fuse panel located in the basement. We spoke with several residents who told us that when the building burned down, the town was rife with gossip that the fire was certainly no accident.

Ramsey Cemetery and Caves

Location: Effingham, Effingham County, Illinois

Directions: Take 33/32 W, it will split—take 32N. Turn right on 2000th Ave. and follow it until it curves to the right and then back to the left and becomes 1975th Ave. Take that until 1230th where you will turn right. About halfway to the cemetery, you will see a small road/trail on your left. There is also a small parking area. This is the trail to the caves.

Ghost Lore

Some of our favorite types of cases are the ones where, not only do you get a spooky haunting, but you get some extra paranormal activity to go along with it. The Ramsey Cemetery and caves is one such case. Although tales of the area's ghostly activity have been circulating for many years, the old cemetery continues to remain hidden deep in the woods, surrounded only by trees, farmland, and caves. But be warned—the surrounding landscape may give you the feeling of being completely alone . . . which is true, if you don't count spirits and werewolves.

- The secluded cemetery is haunted by a troubled young man who ended his life while visiting the cemetery.

- A mysterious hairy creature has been spotting roaming the land around the cemetery and caves. It is believed that the caves serve as its lair.

- Deep within the walking trails is a supernatural hooded man with glowing red eyes.

History

1851 – Twenty-nine-year-old Alexander Ramsey was the first to be buried in a marked grave. Within three years, three more members of the Ramsey family were buried on the land.

1863 – The Ramsey Cemetery was thought to have been officially established. The land that the cemetery rests on was thought to be owned by the Hooten family. According to John Russell's book, *Effingham County, Illinois - Past and Present*, Corporal Henry A. Hooten was a member of Co. K 89th Illinois Infantry Regiment of Effingham. Mr. Hooten is buried in the cemetery.

No one knows if Mr. Hooten donated the land to the town, or if he sold it. For some unknown reason, the cemetery was named after the Ramsey family and not the Hooten family. It is believed that because Ramsey was the first known grave and the Ramsey family owned a successful mill, that the cemetery was named after them.

1920s – A small chapel sat on the cemetery grounds. The chapel was mainly used to provided shelter from the weather for mourners during funerals.

1950-60s – Many visitors began to vandalize and damage the chapel. The chapel was finally torn down because of the damage.

Investigation

The stories of the caves and cemetery being haunted have been around for many years. Several senior women told us that when they were kids in the 1940s, mischievous boys would try to lure girls out to the caves and cemetery in order to scare them with ghost stories.

Several sources we talked with told of a suicide that took place in the chapel. The story goes that one dark evening in the 1960s, a troubled young man drove out to the chapel. Once there he grabbed a shot gun from the trunk of his car, walked inside the chapel and blew his head off. The last name of the man was said to be Bartimus. Due to the Illinois Privacy Law regarding death records, we were unable to search for the man's death certificate.

Another version of the story states that one evening the young man drove out to the chapel by himself. He took a rope from his car, tied it around his neck and walked into the chapel. The next day his lifeless body was found hanging at the end of a rope.

It appears that many curious people often traveled to the cemetery late at night in hopes of encountering a ghost. A woman stated that during summer evenings she used to go to the cemetery with a group of friends and watch for the ghosts that were said to roam the cemetery and caves.

The cemetery sexton is in charge of maintaining the cemetery. He has heard many stories of people encounters spirits while visiting the cemetery. While on the job, he has personally encountered many weird things. On one occasion, he was walking toward the back of the cemetery when he stumbled upon a gruesome discovery. Pinned to one of the old trees was the bloody body of a crucified possum. The sexton also reported that numerous times he has found strange symbols and offerings hanging from the cemetery trees.

In addition to the cemetery, many weird stories have been told about the series of caves that surround the cemetery. Many people that we spoke with had heard stories describing an unusual creature that inhabits the caves. Witnesses say that the creature is a large werewolf, and that it uses the caves as its lair to drag back its unfortunate prey.

The caves themselves are also said to be haunted by several ghosts and spirits. The most commonly reported ghost is that of a strange hooded man. Those who see him say that he will pierce you with his glowing red eyes. We were unable to find any historical cases of this unusual man in the area.

Haunted Bridge and Cemetery

Location: Falmouth, Jasper County, Illinois

Directions: From Hwy 133N take the Falmouth turn-off. Follow 1400 N. It makes a small break but continues as 1400 N. Just before the bottom of the large hill there will be a gravel road on your right hand side. Take this road to the cemetery. The bridge is located at the bottom of the large hill.

Ghost Lore

The area around Love Ford Bridge is a popular hang-out spot for young partiers looking to enjoy themselves far away from the prying eyes of adults and the police. Tucked away in a valley overlooking the Embarrass River, the area is almost completely surrounded by dense forests. For many years the area has enjoyed the reputation of being a great place to party and unwind. That reputation has attracted curious people from all over the region who travel to the area for the sole purpose of having a fun time. However, many visitors often get more than they bargained for, as they soon come to find out that the area also has a long reputation of being haunted.

- The spirits of those who have drowned in the river continue to haunt the area.

- On top of the hill there is a remote cemetery where phantom balls of light have been seen floating among the gravestones.

- Those brave enough to visit the cemetery experience unexplainable cold spots while walking by the gravestones.

History

1955 – Cleon Culp was born.

1975 – Cleon was found dead in the Embarrass River.

2005 – The old bridge was replaced with a new modern bridge by the Wade Township.

Investigation

The cemetery located off the top of the hill is Higgins Cemetery.

Talking with many older residents in town, we are fairly certain that the Embarrass River has claimed several victims over the years. We were able to confirm one death caused by the river. It happened on Friday, April 25th, 1975, when Cleon Culp was enjoying himself at a large party that was held at the bridge. Witnesses claim that Cleon had consumed quite a bit of alcohol and several types of drugs during the party. Apparently the drugs worked, because at approximately 10:30 p.m. Cleon announced to the 200 partygoers that he was a butterfly and could float through the air. He then climbed up on the side of the bridge, and before his friends could stop him, he dove into the dark waters below. After searching the river for nearly two weeks, authorities finally found Cleon's lifeless body.

A young man told us that he was out near the river one evening when he heard strange noises coming from the river. At first the noises sounded like several kids playing and splashing around in

the murky river. Because it was so cold outside, the witness thought that it was highly unlikely that anyone would be swimming in the frigid river. Yet, as he got closer to the river, the sounds got louder. When he finally reached the bridge, he looked down into the water and was shocked to see several ghostly figures floating in the water.

Another legend of the area claims that on dark moonless evenings, many satanic rituals have taken place at the cemetery. One young man reported that when he visited the cemetery, he discovered a small noose, which was stained red, hanging from a tree. Other residents have heard gruesome tales of small animal sacrifices being performed near the cemetery. We were unable to find any evidence of satanic activity.

We spoke to several residents who were bored one evening and decided to gather some friends and drive out to the cemetery. While walking through the cemetery, they were overcome with the uneasy sense that they were not alone. Just then, the group spotted an orb of light floating across one of the graves. Determined to figure out what they had just seen, they started to move closer to the light. As they cautiously took a few more steps, the orb simply vanished before their eyes.

IOOF Cemetery

Location: Granite City, Madison County, Illinois

Directions: From Pontoon road turn toward the Wal-Mart. Turn right in front of Wal-Mart on Schaffer Rd. Follow road and the IOOF Cemetery will be on your right. Make sure to drive slow, as the cemetery is overgrown and hard to spot.

Ghost Lore

Hidden off to the side of the passing road sits the Odd Fellows Cemetery. When you first enter the graveyard, you discover that the cemetery has seen better days. Overrun with scattered brush, fallen trees, and a healthy supply of weeds, it looks like nothing out of the ordinary takes place here. Yet, buried in this cemetery lies the nearly forgotten grave of a woman named Lucinda. Not content with resting in eternal bliss, Lucinda spends her nights rising from the dead to terrorize those foolish enough to pass by the cemetery gates.

- A cursed spirit roams the nearby streets that surround the cemetery.

- If you enter the cemetery at night for any other reason than to mourn the death of an Irish family member, an angry spirit of the Irish family will make sure that your first visit to the cemetery will be your last.

- Many unsuspecting visitors have been scared to death while exploring the cemetery.

- A family member of Daniel Boone is buried inside the cemetery.

History

1801 – The area was settled with immigrants from Ireland.

1830 – Lucinda Elliot was born.

1833 – Lucinda moved to the area with her parents.

1848 – Lucinda's parents moved out of the area while Lucinda decided to stay. It is thought that she stayed because she had fallen in love with Tyler Irish.

1841 – The first burial was believed to have been Jacob Job.

1851 – The Odd Fellow Lodge #87 established the cemetery.

1893 – Lucinda's husband Tyler Irish passed away from a buggy accident while checking on patients.

1895 – Lucinda passed away. The cause of death is unknown.

1895-1900 – A road was constructed through the cemetery only a few inches from the graves of Lucinda and Tyler Irish.

1960s – Many of the gravestones were destroyed or broken by vandals.

1981 – Darlene Hatcher inventoried the cemetery.

1983 – Mary Jane Glass published an inventory with the *Madison County Genealogical Society Cemetery Book.*

1992 – Brush and trees were cleared from the site. Orville Hommert gathered additional information on those buried in the cemetery.

Sources: *Granite City IL Cemeteries* by Mary Jane Gass, Orville Hommert, and Kate Hommert. "The Legend of Lucinda's Graveyard" by Sharon Jones.

Investigation

The cemetery is also known as the Irish Cemetery and the Old Confederate Cemetery. The gravestone of Lucinda is still inside the cemetery.

The surname of the person believed to be a family member of Daniel Boone is not Boone, and the family is said to have moved to California.

Lucinda Elliot moved to the area from Jersey County, Illinois, with her family. She quickly fell in love with handsome young man named Tyler Irish. When Lucinda's family decided to move away, Lucinda opted to stay and pursue her love. Her gamble on love paid off, as she and Tyler were soon married.

According to the article, "Lucinda's Graveyard" by Sharon Jones, the legend of the cemetery haunting dates back many years. Lucinda's spirit was first disturbed from her eternal sleep when residents unwisely constructed a road that ran right through the burial ground. The sound of horse hoofs clacking against the ground, along with the cloud of dust kicked up from slow moving buggies, insured that Lucinda could never again rest peacefully in her grave.

Workers at a nearby factory working the late-night shift have reported seeing a mysterious figure of a woman floating through the fields that border the cemetery.

We spoke with young couple that visited the cemetery one evening to catch a glimpse of Lucinda's spirit. Although they did not see the ghost of Lucinda, they heard the sound of people talking inside the cemetery even though they could not see anyone around. Not wanting to find out if the dare was true, the couple exited the cemetery a quick as possible.

The Dare. If you visit the cemetery at night without the intentions of paying respect to the Irish family, a vengeful spirit of that family will appear to you and your life will be taken from you as you pass away from fright.

House of Plenty

Location: Highland, Madison County, Illinois
Address: 802 Ninth Street, Highland, IL 62249-1522
Phone: (618) 654-4868
Email: hhop@hometel.com

Directions: From 160, turn north on Walnut St. Turn left on 9th St. and the restaurant will be on your right side.

Ghost Lore

Tucked away off the main street in this sleepy rural town rests the historic Grauz Home. Most people know the place as the House of Plenty restaurant, and for the past twenty years the restaurant has been known throughout the area for its friendly service and delicious home cooked food. Yet, over the years the restaurant has also established a haunted reputation where visitors may get a glimpse of the paranormal while eating their pie.

- The main story tells of the restaurant being haunted by the ghost of its original owner, who eternally waits for the return of his friends who met their fate away at sea.

- The mysterious apparition of a man dressed from the early 1900s has been spotted roaming the hallways of the restaurant.

- For several decades, various objects in the house have simply vanished into thin air and have never been found again.

- An elderly woman who once lived in the building came back to visit and tour her old family home. Her visit did not last long, as she was soon overcome by her haunted memories of the building and had to quickly leave the restaurant.

History

1879 – The home was built as a residence for Timothy Grauz.

Throughout the years only three families have owned the home. Past owners of the home include Gerald Moser, George Reinhardt, and David Loyet.

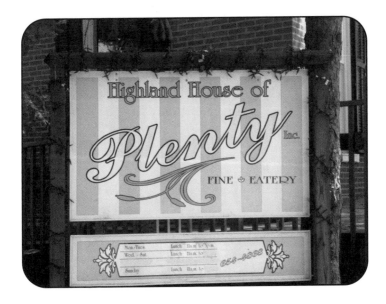

Early 1980s – Ken and Judy Ernst rented part of the building to use as a small bakery for Judy to bake and sell her goods.

Mid-1980s – With business expanding the Ernsts decided to purchase the home. Their goal was to live in part of the home, while using the remainder of the building as a small restaurant business with just a few tables.

Late 1980s – With business continuing to grow, the Ernsts expanded the restaurant throughout the entire building. The family moved out of the home and into a different home in the country.

Currently – The Ernsts are looking to retire and have placed the restaurant up for sale.

Investigation

According to an article by Dawn Vogel in the *Highland News Leader,* the home is thought to be haunted by Timothy Grauz. The story goes that years ago Mr. Grauz hosted a festive party in his

home for the community's early Swiss settlers, who were sailing back to Switzerland to visit their families. Unfortunately, tragedy struck the travelers when their shipped sank in the sea, taking the lives of over 300 passengers. Some believe that after losing so many friends in the accident, the spirit of Mr. Grauz continues to await their return, even from the afterlife.

We spoke with several staff members who informed us that while working in the restaurant, they had often seen kitchen items fly across the room as though they were thrown by some unseen force.

One day the owners were hauling equipment upstairs when they heard the sound of whistling coming from their yard. Believing that their son was outside making the noise, the couple went about their routine as though nothing had happened. Yet, as the whistling noise got louder, the couple decided to investigate. Once outside, they noticed that their son was not anywhere to be found. They finally found the boy inside the house where he too was trying to track down the mysterious whistling.

Back when the owners lived in the building, they reported many strange events taking place in their bedroom. At night the owners would turn off their bedroom light and hop into bed. On several occasions while laying down, the bedroom light would mysteriously turn on by itself, and the couple would have to get up and shut it off again. Thinking that the phenomenon was caused by faulty wiring, the couple finally brought in an electrician to solve the problem. The electrician checked the wiring of the entire house, which had been replaced and could offer no explanation for the strange events.

One day the owner was baking an angel food cake in the kitchen. When she finished putting the final touches on the cake, she left it on the counter to cool. Several hours later she came back to retrieve the cooled cake, only to find that it had simply vanished. Neither the cake nor the pan was ever found.

The owner thought the missing cake and pan was an isolated event until she received an unexpected visit from a woman who had once lived in the home with her mother. The curious visitor asked the owner if she had ever had anything go missing. While being told

the story of the missing cake and pan, the visitor turned a ghostly white. The visitor then told the story of the bizarre incident that happened to her mother while in the house. Years ago her mother had been boiling potatoes on the stove when her husband came home. Her mother went into the living room to greet him and then quickly returned to the kitchen to retrieve the potatoes. The mother was amazed to find that the pot of boiling potatoes had simply vanished without a trace.

Several months later the woman retuned. This time she had brought her 90-year-old mother along, who wanted to see her old house once again and enjoy a meal. Once inside the home the mother immediately wanted to hear the owner's story of the missing cake and pan. When the owner finished telling the puzzling story, the elderly woman was visibly shaken and scared and demanded to leave the building at once.

Throughout the restaurant, many people have spotted a figure of a man walking in the hallway. The man is described as being dressed as though he is from the early 1900s.

Inside the dining room sits an old fireplace. Located next to the fireplace are several large tables for the guests. Each year around Christmas, the owners would witness a strange phenomenon take place in this area. The owner would walk by the tables and notice a pile of charred pipe tobacco on the corner. The family was extremely puzzled as to how the tobacco could have gotten on the table. Their answer seemed to come when a former occupant of the home brought in an old picture of the original owners of the home. Standing in the picture was a young man smoking a tobacco pipe. The man was identified as the son of the original owner. It is believed that the son loved to smoke his pipe while sitting next to the fireplace at night.

We spoke with the owner who informed us that when he first moved into the home he was a skeptic and did not believe in ghosts. Yet after 20 years of personal experiences at the restaurant, he is now thoroughly convinced that ghosts exist.

Phantom Roses of Lakeview Cemetery

Location: Johnston City, Williamson County, Illinois
Address: 100 West Broadway Boulevard, Johnston City, IL 62951-1424
Phone: (618) 983-8495

Directions: Take Broadway St. towards Arrowhead Lake as it turns into Corinth. Turn left on Old Frankfort Rd. and the cemetery will be on your right.

Ghost Lore

By now you expect to hear stories of ghosts and spirits roaming around cemeteries. In this book you have numerous chances to visit a haunted cemetery, but you only have one opportunity to visit a cemetery with phantom roses. The legend states that inside the gates of Lakeview Cemetery rests the "Hook Tomb." When you visit the tomb, you will smell the lovely scent of phantom roses.

The only catch is that you need to run around the tomb three times and then knock on the door three times before the smell of phantom roses is emitted.

Locals tell that the smell of phantom roses comes from the ghost of Mr. Hook, who is leaving the flowers for his eternal bride. Other versions state that the grieving ghosts of Mr. and Mrs. Hook are leaving phantom flowers for their child that died as an infant.

History

1911 – According to council meetings on file at City Hall, the cemetery committee gathered to plan the City Cemetery. The committee reported that they had discovered a tract of 21 acres that belonged to Mr. John Huck. The land was available for purchase at a cost of $175 per acre.

1911 – The association paid out expenses for the mowing, surveying, hauling stone, and cleaning of the cemetery.

1911 – Con Mornaway was appointed the first sexton of the new City Cemetery. His salary was to be $40 a month.

1912 – The first plots of the cemetery were sold at a cost ranging from $1 to $10. The cost of digging the graves was $3, $6, or $7, depending on the size of the grave.

1914 – Con Mornaway was doing such a good job as the sexton of the City Cemetery, his salary was raised from $40 a month to $60 a month.

1918 – The cemetery association voted to purchase a strip of land that sat between the City Cemetery and the road.

1919 – According to the *Marion Daily Republican,* 76 graves were dug during the year. In the previous eight years, 561 graves had been dug.

1933 – E. S. Pike and his wife deeded five acres of land to the City Cemetery for $700. This land served as the new south addition of the cemetery.

1951 – According to the *Marion Daily Republican,* the local Woman's Club sponsored a contest to re-name City Cemetery. The winning name was "Lakeview" which was submitted by three people: Mrs. Minnie Duncan, Mrs. Mon Hudgens, and Ben Blair. Thirty other names were submitted, but were not chosen. Among them were End of the Trail and Bones Place.

Unknown – No one seems to know the exact date the Hook tomb was constructed, but several residents remember hearing that materials for the tomb were brought in on a horse and carriage and that the tomb was assembled completely by hand.

Investigation

We know that the bizarre story of the phantom roses has been in the area for a long time. Local residents remember hearing the stories back in the 1950s, and it may go back even further.

For years people have traveled to the Hook Tomb to explore the legend. While there, the air would mysteriously fill with the scent of roses.

We spoke with a woman who moved to the area with her family in the 1960s. She recalled her children going down to the cemetery to test out the legend of the phantom roses. About an hour later the children came running into the house screaming, "the legend is true, the legend is true."

So what is the cause for the rose smell? Two different versions of the legend have been circulating for years. The first states that when Mr. and Mrs. Hook were still alive, their young child passed away. They built the tomb in his remembrance, and even after death they continue to decorate his grave with roses. The other version tells of the ghost of Mr. Hook coming back from the afterlife to shower the body of his eternal bride with flowers.

Caretakers of the cemetery have their own theory for the phenomenon. They reported that years ago the Hook family would often bring roses to decorate the tomb. They would place the roses inside the tomb, and when visitors would run around the tomb it would create a vacuum that would essentially suck the rose fragrance through the tomb's windows into the outside air.

The Dare. While at the tomb, if you run around the structure three times and then knock on the tomb's door three times, the outside air with fill with the mysterious scent of phantom roses.

Lakey's Ghost

Location: McLeansboro, Hamilton County, Illinois

Directions: Take 14 E out of town for approximately 1.5 miles. Here you will see the bridge that runs over Lakey's Creek. Lakey's cabin is thought to have been located north of the creek.

Ghost Lore

Thanks to Washington Irvin's story, *The Legend of Sleepy Hollow,* the idea of a headless horseman riding through the woods is universally known. Irving sets his fictional story in a small Dutch settlement in New York. However, those passing over Lakey's Creek in McLeanboro believe that the headless horseman lives not in New York, but in their own backyard.

- The headless ghost of Mr. Lakey roams the countryside looking for justice and revenge for his murder so many years ago.

- A headless ghost riding a mysterious large black horse accompanies anyone traveling through the land.

History

1821 – According to researcher Geneva Nipper, the town of McLeansboro was laid out. The town was named after William B. McLean, who donated 20 acres of land. McLean was to get the money for one-third of the lots sold.

1821 – William Hall received a contract for the sum of $780 to build a jail for the town.

1827 – It is believed that the Methodists were the first group to set up prayer meetings in the town.

1830 – The town constructed a fire-proof brick courthouse.

1830s – Court records show a Lakey's Creek.

1853 – The town agreed to build a Masonic lodge. Prior to this decision, many townsfolk belonged to the lodge in Mt. Vernon.

1855 – The first county newspaper was started called the *Hamilton News.*

1856 – The town got a chapter of the International Organization of Odd Fellows. The group had six charter members: M. M. Young, Lorenzo Rathbone, Charles Gilman, John W. Oneal, Chester Carpenter, and D. F. Asbury.

1869 – A fire-proof building was constructed at a cost of approximately $7,000. The building was to be used for offices.

1874 – The town suffered a terrible fire. The fire destroyed the area known as Walker's Block. The fire was discovered during the evening, and the cause of the fire was thought to be a cigar that was thrown into some wood shavings.

1877 – The town constructed a new school house out of brick. It was the first school house in town to be made of brick.

1894 – The town's first fire department was organized.

1901 – The first rural delivery of mail in McLeansboro took place.

1938 – The present courthouse was constructed.

Source: John B. Kinnear- *McLeansboro Times,* February 7, 1884

Investigation

People have been telling the legend of Lakey's Creek for many decades. The legend tells of a man named known as Lakey. Lakey was said to own a piece of land near a small creek that ran through the area. John Allen, in his book, *Legends & Lore of Southern*

Illinois, writes that Lakey was in the process of constructing a beautiful log cabin on his land. After weeks of long hard-working days, Lakey was nearly finished building his cabin. Lakey only needed to cut down one last tree to put the finishing touches on his home. After downing the tree, Lakey decided to retired for the evening, with his dream of finishing his home only one day away. Unfortunately, Lakey would never get a chance to finish his cabin, because the very next morning a traveler stumbled on to the horrific scene. There before the traveler's eyes, next to a large stump, laid Lakey's decapitated body. Lakey's bloody head was found several feet away. A short distance from the body was Lakey's axe covered in blood and stuck into a stump. Visitors to the gruesome site said that there were no signs of a struggle. The townsfolk were baffled as to who would have killed Lakey as he was well liked, wasn't wealthy, and seemed to have no enemies.

The next day Lakey's decapitated body was buried near his cabin. But his spirit did not rest long. The following evening two men were riding through the area of Lakey's cabin when they were joined by a strange companion. Both travelers saw a headless man

riding a large black steed, moving with them from the other side of the creek. Neither man had the nerve to make a sound, as they pressed forward with greater speed. As the travelers neared the center of the creek, the headless rider turned to the left and seemed to simply melt into the water.

Allen also writes that after finally losing the headless rider, the two terrified men rode home as fast as they could. The witnesses were hesitant to share their story with anyone, afraid that others may think they were crazy. However, a few evenings later two additional men were passing by the creek when they had an eerie encounter with the same phantom rider.

For years townsfolk would often hear stories of unsuspecting visitors being accompanied by the headless rider as they passed through the area.

The real identity of Mr. Lakey is still unknown. Most of the stories in current ghost books and paranormal websites list him only as a man called Lakey.

Records show that a Joel Lakey purchased a plot of land in the area in 1815.

The census of 1818 lists that a Simon Lakey and his wife were living in the area.

A court record of 1819 shows that Simon Lakey went to court on charges of trespassing. Yet by the time of the 1820 census, no one by the name of Lakey was living in the area.

We found an account of the death of Mr. Lakey from a book dating back to 1887. We are unsure as if this was the same Lakey or not. According to the book, *The History of Gallatin, Saline, Hamilton, Franklin, and Williamson Counties, Illinois,* Lakey's Creek was named after Mr. Lakey who lived on the "Jones tract" of land and was killed by his son in law. The records not state the name of the son in law, but researcher Ralph Harrelson believes the "Jones tract" of land was owned by a Michael Jones of Shawneetown.

We spoke with a woman who had seen the ghost of the headless horseman. The woman was well acquainted with the legend of Lakey's Creek, as she passed by the area daily on her commute to work. On evening while returning home from work, the woman noticed something moving in the woods near the creek. As the woman slowed down to get a better look at what she had seen, she almost crashed her car because of what was staring back at her. Perched on top of a large horse was a man with no head. The woman reported that the headless rider looked like a real person, just without a head. The woman did not stop to find out what the rider was as she sped off toward home.

Phantom Funeral of Fort de Chartres

Location: Prairie du Rocher, Randolph County, Illinois
Address: Fort de Chartres Historic Site, 1350 State Route 155, Prairie du Rocher, IL 62277-2006
Phone & Fax: (618) 284-7230
Email: ftdchart@htc.net
Website: www.ftdechartres.com

Directions: Take Hwy 155 W for four miles past Prairie du Rocher, and you will come to the historic fort.

Ghost Lore

The Historic Fort de Chartres rests peacefully near the small quiet town of Prairie du Rocher. The unique history of the fort is what attracts thousands of visitors to its door every year. Yet even with the fort's rich history, which is filled with murder and tragedy, the fort is best known as being the home of an infamous funeral.

Thousands of funerals take place every single day, so what makes the fort's funeral any different? Well, the answer to that question is simple—the funeral procession, that witnesses see pass by the old fort, is a phantom funeral!

Every year in which July 4th falls on a Friday, the dead will arise, and a phantom funeral will make an appearance.

History

1673 – The French claimed the Illinois land for France.

1718 – A contingent of men was sent to the area to establish a civil government in the area.

1720 – French soldiers began construction of the wooden fort.

1725 – Work on a new, more modern fort began.

1742 – The run-down fort was in severe need of major repairs and upgrades.

1753-56 – The wooden fort was renovated with limestone to help stabilize and protect the fort.

1760 – Louisiana's fiscal officer reported that the fort would be done by the years end.

1763 – The French soldiers surrendered the fort to Great Britain.

1765 – British troops took control of the fort and a large ceremony took place to honor the event.

1765 – The British decided to re-name the fort. The new name of the fort was Fort Cavendish.

1771 – The British thought the fort was of little value and abandoned it.

1772 – The fort's south wall and bastions collapsed into the Mississippi River.

1800s – The fort was run down and severely dilapidated. Much of the material of the fort was stolen by locals in search of supplies.

1900 – Above ground, no part of the original wall existed.

1913 – The Illinois legislature decided to purchase the fort for the use as a state park.

1917 – The state restored part of the fort, including the historic powder magazine.

1920s – The Works Administration reconstructed many of the buildings that had once sat on the land.

1936 – The main gateway of the fort was restored by the National Society Daughters of American Colonists and by the State of Illinois.

1993 – A great flood damaged the fort. Both staff and volunteers refurbished the site after the flood.

Investigation

The fort was named in honor of Louis duc de Chartres, who was the son of the regent of France. The fort's historic powder magazine is considered to be the oldest building in the State of Illinois.

The main paranormal story that surrounds the fort involves the phantom funeral procession. It is said that on every July 4th that falls on a Friday, the dead will rise from the earth and partake in a phantom funeral.

The first glimpse of this strange funeral was believed to have taken place in 1889. In his book *Legends and Lore of Southern Illinois,* John Allen writes of a sighting that took place on the evening of July 4th, 1889. It was here that a woman named Mrs. Chris and her neighbor went out to sit on the front porch in order to escape the heat of house. It was nearly midnight, and the women sat talking quietly, cooling off in the moon-filled night. The neighbor looked out at the road and was shocked to see a funeral procession going by, and asked Mrs. Chris if she, too, could see it. Mrs. Chris stat-

ed that she also saw the funeral. At first glance, the funeral did not seem that odd, as a small cemetery was located right down the road from the house. Yet both women thought it was a weird time for a funeral. As they stared intently at the wagons passing by, the weirdness began. Even though the funeral was made up of a casket, 40 horse-drawn wagons, and thirteen pairs of horseman, no noise could be heard. The women said they saw horse hoofs hit the ground, wagon wheels spitting up dust on the gravel, and the mourners seemed to be talking, yet not a single sound broke the silent night air. The women also got more than a fading glimpse of the funeral, as they reported the eerie funeral seemed to take over an hour to pass by them.

By this time the women were completely baffled by the mystery they had just witnessed. Determined to get to the bottom of it, the women vowed to sit and wait on the porch to see if anyone returned from the cemetery after they buried the deceased. However, the women were even more perplexed when the funeral procession never came back. The next day, while searching for others that may have also witnessed the strange event, the neighbor discovered that her father had also seen the phantom funeral. The father had stepped outside to see what the family dog was howling at, when he, too, spotted the mysterious funeral going by.

It is believed that the witnesses in 1889 had seen a real funeral that had taken place many years ago. Due to a horrific murder, on every July 4th that happens to fall on a Friday, the funeral procession is cursed to rise from the earth and march its ghostly way to the hidden cemetery.

There are several different origins as to the death that causes the phantom funeral. Allen wrote that many years prior to 1889, a man of some importance was killed in an ambush in order to prevent him from continuing his work. The authorities told the killers that to avoid detection, the corpse must be buried in an obscure cemetery using only the light of the moon.

Researcher Troy Taylor writes of another version of the story involving the murder of a man for the love of a woman. In 1765, two officers from rival armies fought over the affections of a young local woman. In the end the British officer was killed and the murderer, a French officer, escaped downriver to avoid prosecution. The authorities were afraid that if word of the officer's death got out it would provoke even more bloodshed so they order that his body be buried in secret.

We interviewed several staff of the fort who knew the details of the phantom funeral procession but had never witnessed the funeral themselves. The employees did tell us that other strange events happen at the fort. Employees report hearing strange noises while working at the site, yet no source can be found.

Several visitors to the historic fort told us that when they visited the fort they got a feeling of not being alone. They got the feeling that they were being watched while touring the site.

About the Authors

Chad Lewis is a paranormal investigator for Unexplained Research LLC, with a Master's Degree in Applied Psychology from the University of Wisconsin-Stout. He has spent years traveling the globe researching ghosts, strange creatures, crop formations, werewolves, and UFOs. Chad is a former State Director for the Mutual UFO Network and has worked with BLT Crop Circle Investigations. He is the organizer of the Unexplained Conferences and the host of *The Unexplained* paranormal radio talk show.

Terry Fisk is also a paranormal investigator for Unexplained Research LLC and an authority on death and the afterlife. He is a shamanic Buddhist practitioner and member of the Foundation for Shamanic Studies who studied philosophy and religion at the University of Wisconsin. Terry is the co-host of *The Unexplained* paranormal radio talk show and director for *The Unexplained* television series.

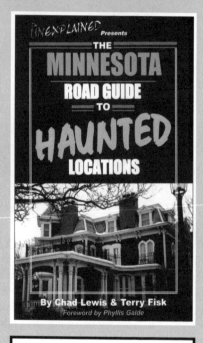